One Man's Maine: Essays on a Love Affair

One Man's Maine

Essays on a Love Affair

Jim Krosschell

Illustrated by Emma Krosschell

GREEN WRITERS PRESS
Brattleboro, Vermont

Printed in the United States

10 9 8 7 6 5 4 3 2 1

Green Writers Press is a Vermont-based publisher whose mission is to spread
a message of hope and renewal through the words and images we publish.
Throughout we will adhere to our commitment to preserving and protecting
the natural resources of the earth. To that end, a percentage of our proceeds
will be donated to environmental activist groups and Coastal Mountains Land
Trust in Maine. Green Writers Press gratefully acknowledges support from
individual donors, friends, and readers to help support the environment
and our publishing initiative.

Giving Voice to Writers & Artists Who Will Make the World a Better Place
Green Writers Press | Brattleboro, Vermont
www.greenwriterspress.com

Library of Congress Cataloging-in-Publication Data available upon request.

ISBN: 978-0-9982604-2-6

COVER PHOTO: RICHARD SCHULTZ PHOTOGRAPHY
www.rschultz.com

PRINTED ON PAPER WITH PULP THAT COMES FROM FSC-CERTIFIED FORESTS, MANAGED FORESTS THAT GUARANTEE
RESPONSIBLE ENVIRONMENTAL, SOCIAL, AND ECONOMIC PRACTICES BY LIGHTNING SOURCE ALL WOOD PRODUCT
COMPONENTS USED IN BLACK & WHITE, STANDARD COLOR, OR SELECT COLOR PAPERBACK BOOKS, UTILIZING EITHER
CREAM OR WHITE BOOKBLOCK PAPER, THAT ARE MANUFACTURED IN THE LAVERGNE, TENNESSEE PRODUCTION
CENTER ARE SUSTAINABLE FORESTRY INITIATIVE® (SFI®) CERTIFIED SOURCING

*In homage to E.B. White, whose delight
in the ordinary, compassion in the face of chaos,
and comfort in his own skin can only
be imitated, never equaled.*

Contents

One Man's Maine: Essays on a Love Affair

Berries

NOT QUITE TEENAGERS, the children were noncommittal when I sat on the grass next to the deck and picked weeds: no sidelong glances, no eye-rolling, no sliding into fast French as they would do later. There was no particular reason to weed—the lawn was hopeless—but they knew that time was precious on vacation, and adults did what they had to do, and the girls weren't going to interfere.

They didn't know it was therapeutic to sit in the sun in the middle of the day and tame a few square feet of world, to marvel at the proliferation of plantain and fleabane, to pull at a root and see its young runner wiggle six inches away and comb through the grasses to pluck it out. For a few weeks that patch of lawn would be satisfyingly bare, a few tufts of grass looking not much better than weeds, to be honest, but free of interference and liberated for growth; next year the patch would be exactly as weedy as before, and that would be comforting too, as if at least something hadn't changed while the children had.

In the sleepy period right after lunch, while they and my wife lounged on the deck above me and decided on the outing for the day, their rosy cheeks and blonde hair shining in the sun like precious fruits ripening, weeding was the perfect thing to do. In the morning we read our novels and tried to forget about competitor analyses and five-year plans and deadlines, the girls sleeping late, watching videos, tolerating lunch so quickly on the heels of breakfast, until the decision for the afternoon was made and suddenly they had to move: "C'mon, Daddy! Let's go!"

"I'm coming," I'd say, torn between their going and my staying, and when at last we tumbled into the van, menacingly I waved my fingers stained with dandelion juice and they stuck their bare feet into the space between the front seats and I pretended (hoped) to mark them for life.

After the beach or the hike, we gathered in the Adirondack chairs down by the shore. The same weeds grew here except there were also the red wandering stems of wild strawberries, stunted by the ocean winds, never bearing any fruit, or if they did, we attended school and furthered careers in June and were prevented from seeing them. It didn't matter; strawberries were a grown-up fruit, to be bought at supermarkets or picked at giant farms from orderly rows. They came from our other life, just another purchase in or out of season, flown from Israel for Christmas waffles and birthday shortcake, not for our care-free family time, drinking Kool-Aid in milky plastic bottles and Sea Dog beer and eating chips we bought only in Maine. The weeding of wild berries was nothing about conquering them, it was about tracing the tentative routes of their tiny vines, cultivating their miniature habitats, taking in the prattle of children in love with their lives.

᠉

The raspberry patch at the top of Bay View Terrace was wild and overgrown, belonging to someone and everyone. Tender skin required long pants and bug dope. Tradition required that we use the same red-stained green berry boxes from years past. Children disappeared in the brambles, following the paths already trampled by the invisible community of pickers and complaining about thorns and mosquitoes. Parents worried about snakes and Eastern equine encephalitis, and after an hour or so, when each girl emerged with a dainty half quart, there was bilateral pride and relief. The adults, more hardened, produced full boxes and all together we had enough for one large luscious spoonful each at lunch and then, the highlight of the week, a freshly baked pie that night, glazy-red, sweet, with a touch of worldly sour, that we drooled over until it was cool enough, usually at the end of the first round of Wizard, to eat. We sat around the table in the protective glow of the stained-glass overhead lamp as the night fell so wonderfully slowly in the northern summer, and the sound of the surf through the open French door was like a kiss on the ear. The older daughter, having watched its preparation, ate pie quickly, smacking her lips, and the younger daughter, having helped with the crust, ate slowly and neatly, and the parents sat in waking dreamland, with the saucy taste on our tongues and the suspension of disbelief in our hearts.

We cut the pie in sixths. This is something parents do, moderating, planning, trying to extend the perfect day. At lunch the next day, those two leftover pieces reminded me of my parents. Raspberries must have been some unconscious symbol of everything my father missed in his disciplined and orderly life, so he planted canes behind the shed at our summer cabin in Michigan. The experiment lasted only a year or two before he gave up. At the slightest hint of redness, the deer or the robins got breakfast, and he did not want to get up early enough, or build costly fences—it was summer, he was a struggling school principal—to prevent it. The canes were left to go wild, and eventually disappeared. They provided no memorable family pie.

There *had* been perfect days at that cabin, uncreated, spontaneous. But they were too divorced from reality, or I could say, the reality they were divorced from was all too powerful. We were not prepared to return from heaven at the end of the summer.

I hope for my daughters that raspberries are the symbol of spontaneity. Do not buy them in supermarkets, do not order them from dessert menus in January, naked in winter air and cold. Let them stay tender and fragile and fleeting. Left out in the old green boxes, they grow mold after a day or two. Stashed in the refrigerator, they lose all their taste. Let them grow and ripen without the heavy hand of moderation. Eat the whole pie at once.

Having gone back to our duty-bound lives in the late summer and early fall, we would miss the second crop of raspberries that grew on the edges of the meadow halfway up Bay View. I pick them now when I walk the dog. They are small, more sour than sweet, not hiding under leaves anymore but straining for the last of the sun's rays, a metaphor striving to become a memory, all grown up in the shrunken, adult kind of way.

ॐ

In Maine, blueberries are ubiquitous in August. The roads are thick with stands advertising "Wild Blueberrys." They prop up much of the economy Down East. They are harvested by mechanized rakes. They have big cousins in supermarkets. They are an icon, an industry.

The field where we picked them, down Ash Point Road next to the airport, was open, pricker-free, too sunny for mosquitoes and snakes, exposed to hawks, tourists, and jet-fuel exhaust. By this time of the summer the sun was hot, and hats, not long pants, were required. Backs, young and old, hurt from bending. When a jet roared in, carrying businessmen and tourists from Boston, my stomach clenched and I thought of the trips facing me in the fall.

August in the north country aches with time gained, time lost. But the blueberry grows on, close to the earth, spreading underground, profligate with promise. It creates its own paradise, even through the winter. We filled our green boxes quickly, and the pie we ate that night was luscious in spite of the ubiquity of its berries.

The blueberry field on Ash Point Road has moved on. It was plowed and leveled and is now a second town cemetery. The daughters have moved on also, are college students, working summer jobs, and their parents re-create serendipity elsewhere, in the little patches of blue at the end of the hike up Bald Rock, or sneaking a couple of handfuls from the organic fields of Beech Hill Preserve, or day-dreaming in the supermarket in the cold of January.

ॐ

Most of the way down Bay View sits a curious little tableau. On one side of the road there's a small hut, maybe ten feet by eight, leaning a little, door barely attached and splintered, a playhouse neglected.

Vines and overgrowing shrubs threaten to make it irrelevant. Yet it has three large windows with screens that look to be in good shape; it has dignity and style, with a peaked roof and weathered cedar shakes. With a little love and kindness it could be restored to someone's artistic or childhood vision of happy fantasy.

Across the road on the south side is a rectangular patch of open grass, too small for croquet, about right for badminton. Someone takes the trouble to keep it clear, mowing the grass in summer. Except for a narrow opening, it is lined most of the way around by blackberry bushes.

It's not clear whether the point of the fantasist on this side of the road was the grass or the blackberries. I picture children from a big house on the shore finger-painting or assigning roles in make-believe in the house, then lunching on PB&J and Kool-Aid on the grass. I imagine an artist seizing the slate-blue of the ocean in gesso or glaze, then stretching out in the August sun with a book and a bowl of blackberries and a love of the ordinary. Their ghosts take turns mowing.

There's nothing so ordinary as blackberries. They're hard to get right. My daughters tried them, but unless conditions were perfect, the berries were bland, or sour, and full of seeds. The girls seldom walked with us then, and don't at all anymore, and thus have missed the true blackberry beauty. We take the dog to Lucia Beach, and along the road, haphazardly, commonly, a stray bush leans towards us from its place at the edge of the woods, almost every berry black. It's the moment unanticipated, and I pick handfuls and we taste the surprising sweetness and spit seeds playfully and think about our daughters growing up shielded by love and memory from a world of terror.

‹❧›

Bay View Terrace is a lovely little road, maybe a quarter mile long, almost perfect in its ordinariness. Between Cann's Beach Road to the north and Granite Point Road to the south lie some one hundred acres of woods, broken only by the houses of our neighbors the McIntoshes—parents' and daughter's—and their driveways and wood piles and swing sets plopped in the middle. It's a normal woods, cut by deer paths, not very dense, and quite open now in winter. The trees are brown-black deciduous and green evergreen and white birch, and it's an owlish kind of place although I've seen but one here. There's a meadow halfway down, made flatter and more obvious by the snow, which in summer is overgrown with scrub and fireweed and late blooming raspberries and now is lined with bushes bearing winterberries. They're hardly the luscious raspberries of July, but winterberries taste as good in the eye as raspberries do in the mouth. They relieve the browns and grays of the winter woods; our red sweaters and yellow caps and the little orange collar for the dog that we put on for our walks display against hunters, not depression. We thirst for every bit of color.

Halfway down the road I stop dead, for no particular reason. The dog also freezes, expecting a menace to confront. In the crunching of boots against ice and snow, I've failed to hear the thrilling silence of a woods in winter, so cold that wind is not allowed. Everything in sight is preternaturally clear: flaking birch bark, wisps of sea smoke on the bay, the cliffs of Vinalhaven that I can just barely see through the tree branches. And close: the cold is intimate, a caress on the face, a hug in the lungs, a squeeze on the heart.

The daughters are away. The feeling of their absence is what I imagine the winterberry to be: bittersweet.

Blueberry Hill

THEY'RE ALMOST A CLICHÉ, such iconically named hills in Maine. I have two of them deeply in mind this barren morning the day after Easter. Neither of them is actually named "Blueberry," unlike several others up and down the coast. Their real names are Bald Rock and Beech Hill, also common names in the state; the former is indeed slightly bald, but the latter has suffered centuries of change and now lacks beeches, and trees, altogether. Places have many guises and long histories—Mt. Desert is hardly deserted, your suburban Deer Run Lane hasn't seen wildlife in decades—but their essences don't lie, and I know, even in a cold spring, that these two hills carry a freight of blueberries in spite of their names. And they carry a weight of dreams, especially in April when clouds blast across the sky, looking shapely as thunderheads, and in an hour dissolve into a gray winter fog. The winds, now warm, now cold, ruffle the bay in a patchwork of herringbone. Rain pelts down; the sun comes out minutes later. On the garage the weathervane swirls, helpless to offer guidance. Minute by minute summer approaches and withdraws. I'm dying to be outside, not yet ambitious for a hill, just a walk. If I go now, it will be cold and wet.

That's what the famous Maine summer builds on, the chill and damp and bluster of spring. No wonder summer's so short. This year's shiver of anticipation is worsened by a heraldic week of false summer, a hot sun in March, burst magnolias, bare skin sweating—yet somewhere in Maine, inevitably, snow will fall before the month is up. Oh, April . . . if I could, I'd command the thermometer to stay above fifty for more than ten minutes and the weathervane to stop pointing north and the leaves just to open and grow, damn it. But I'm a human, not a god. My windows don't protect but imprison, and I want them open to the embrace of air.

The only way to transcend the banalities of this sometime redemptive season is to live them. In the late afternoon, showers mostly past, I walk out into April's high-low world and look only low, at bits and pieces, at the grass struggling for green, at showy flowers like crocuses and daffodils, at Dickinson's dreaded robin, at tiny flowers like flag irises and baby blue eyes, at swamp cabbage pushing out of the cold earth like fire. But that's it, everything else is brown and gray, rotting months' worth of it. Things can only wait, green lying within, and I push away any thoughts of the warm world to come, the high places, the mountaintops. The promise is enough for now. I'm intensified enough by air.

As the clouds roil over the bay, I come to the end of the road, to Lucia Beach and its rocks and blue sea and white surf pounding and the granite ledges bordered by evergreens. Here is the steadiness, the surety I crave, the place that looks the same in April and in August, even in January. Winter is behind me yet still seethes in the cold surf.

&

In my world, natural places are the sacraments lost in the culture's evolution from pagan to skeptic. A theologian would call those sacraments visible forms of invisible grace. So do I. Pagan humans used to celebrate hundreds of sacraments—that is, they hardly made distinctions between the religious and the profane. The Catholic Church reduced worship to seven rites, the Protestants to two. Now we're back to hundreds, thousands, shining in catalogs and malls: the purchasing of a lifestyle. The more mysteries we lose, the more materials we buy.

In a way, Beech Hill was baptized by industrialization. Birthed by the ice age, it was a typical low coastal mountain, fully forested with huge white pines and pointed firs and beech, nothing special unless one adores that kind of thing. But the European settlers of New

England believed trees were holy only if exploited, and they professed their faith in sawmills and masts and fuel. The industrial revolution nearly completed the massacre throughout New England, and eventually a rich Philadelphian perhaps seeking penance bought the bare hill and put up a rustic hut that he called the Beech Nut, in which his wife could mount teas and formal Sunday lunches. The hill changed hands; the teahouse slowly decayed; the land was posted and fenced. By the 1980s developers were petitioning the town fathers for permission to build some four hundred houses. Then wealthy people with a different ethic formed a land trust to buy the hill, restore the hut, encourage the grassland habitat, and coax the native blueberries to clone and spread into a working farm.

Today, in an ecstatically endless parade of beautiful places on the coast of Maine, Beech Hill stands out, a bare beacon for sailors on the main, a vista for tourists on the make. The absence of trees has turned out to be a lucky artifact. The Beech Nut hut floats in changing colors: brown and gray and sometimes white in winter; green in spring; the full palette of summer; the amaranth red of blueberry leaves and stems in fall; and then soon enough back to brown. With its sod roof replanted and the stone walls reinforced and the wrap-around porch now safe for visitors again, the house might easily represent the forgiveness of greed. The dirt road that was used to transport building rocks and canapés is now a wide and easy walking trail, just half a mile, twisting around and up the hill and revealing the panorama of sea and mountains and islands a few frames at a time. Many days, especially under the signature blues of summer, scores of people make the climb to that anointing view: to look up and around at an unobstructed, 360-degree panorama, Penobscot Bay in front, the Camden Hills in back, and the surrounding berry fields, such a pleasure to those of us who walk up and nibble at the edges.

People made this place, people use this place. Every August the land trust opens its fields to a day of free-pick, and hundreds of people hunch over, aching just enough, filling their baskets and iconic green boxes as if an entire community were at home on the land again. A man takes his shrieking children into the fields. Soon they become calm, soothed by air and sun and the treasure hunt of berries.

An old woman remembers the fight for this place and smiles at the wind. Every season is a joy, but especially the summer, the contrast of warm sun and cool breeze, bare limbs, ripening fruit. Is this the perfect collaboration between creator and created? The God that allows evil to exist seems far away.

This is the wilderness of ease, the comfort of cultivation. These are the kind of blueberries called wild—the small, intensely flavorful ones we pick ourselves or buy by the quart from roadside stands, not the intensely cultivated, less-than-intensely flavorful high-bush berries, slightly obese, that appear in the winter from Chile and in summer from the wetter parts of the Midwest and Pacific Coast. Low-bush berries are close to us, iconic, symbolic. Yet they too are marketed and hyped. Can something called wild also be clichéd? Yes, and to each word's greater glory. Somewhere in the Great North Woods black bears are the berry's only customer, but mostly now the wild blueberry is managed, not quite as baldly as corn, say, but certainly to the extent that it is now only partly wild: humans help it along by clearing fields, pruning or burning every other year, spraying herbicides, importing bee colonies to maximize pollination. In gratitude, the plants spread underground, cloning themselves sometimes hundreds of yards away from their mothers.

The harvest on Beech Hill is only a small slice of the pie, so to speak, mostly for privileged coastal dwellers paying higher organic prices. Commercial harvesting of the vast barrens of northern Maine and Atlantic Canada requires the importation of migrant workers using hand rakes. A man or woman bends over some of the hardest farm work known, for nine or ten hours a day, for a month straight, for perhaps ten cents a pound, nearly a thousand berries to the pound. It's a difficult job, but let me hope it's not degrading to him, except for the pay, let me hope she's not the kind of woman who measures her worth by wealth, that she loves her family around her and the wide open sky and the sun setting behind the mountains to the west and the blessed lack of screens—plasma, tablet, smart—in their plywood hut at night. I look at their lives romantically and painfully, but even that is being taken away from them, and the glasses through which we view such a way of life will soon be completely rosy. The camaraderie and the community are giving way to big picking machines, which take over the most productive fields—the levelest, the least rocky—and leave the rest to fewer and fewer, less and less valuable, human harvesters. Hype demands quantity, hype demands nostrums. A carefully crafted touristic view will fix our unhealthy souls. A serving of the wondrous phytochemicals in the "bright" foods will heal our unhealthy bodies. Both true if practiced on, both false if dabbled in.

Beech Hill is the kind of wildness—beautiful, managed, protected—on which whole essays, books, philosophies, livelihoods depend. It is safe enough to exploit. It plays well in glossy magazines. It can indeed redeem us if we work at it.

⚘

Hike up to Bald Rock for a different kind of cure, a purer Eucharist of the gods. The walk is longer this time, a mile and a half through the protected woods of a state park. The trail starts at a small parking lot, goes up a blocked-off dirt road, mostly straight, gradually rising, but then it branches off at the ruined foundation of a cabin. That's the last human spoor. The track becomes narrow, steep, and rocky. The woods are thick and give away no view until the very end, where slivers of bare granite ledge on the summit offer places to sit and gaze out on the bay, across the Fox Islands and Deer Isle and all the way to Acadia. I don't look around; here I'm not at the center of any panorama. One looks only outward on Bald Rock.

Yet this is no Great North Woods wilderness. There is cell phone service, but that doesn't bother the hawks soaring in the thermals or the little patches of blueberries in the sodded hollows of the ledge, it bothers only me. I took friends to climb Bald Rock once. At the top one noticed a missed cell phone call, and spent fifteen minutes tracking it down to a distant acquaintance who had dialed in error.

Enough hikers climb Bald Rock that ripe berries seldom bless my visits, but even if no human ever came here, the plants available would work hard to fill a handful. They have not been coaxed by humans to proliferate. Yet when a ripe berry or two does escape attention, there is nothing like the burst of wild antioxidants on the tongue, at the top of a mountain, in the summer, in Maine. Even in cell-phone range it's a primitive feeling, a connection to underground roots and runners, to a way of life and a plant not built for the convenience of bipeds. How sacred we could feel in real wilderness.

The blueberry is not spectacularly beautiful except close-up, but it stands for what we lack, the ability to be close and humble, on our knees, and its cultivation is like mimicking mystics as they imagine death, their essences spreading eternally through dirt and root.

✤

The rolling blueberry barrens of Washington County are well named. Unlike humans and their constructs, the blueberry erects no protections against difficult circumstances; indeed, it thrives in hot sun, poor soils, and the bad weather of a perpetual April Down East. It accepts glacial boulders and erratics in its path, creeping around them. It offers humans a month of employment in one of the poorest places in the country. A few tourists come but are unlikely to build second homes on land that can produce two tons of fruit an acre. The land is only slightly improvable. We are not tempted to clear-cut the barrens. They would be beautiful even if we didn't help the blueberries along a bit.

Most constructs of man are not "beautiful." They may be stunning, or striking, but airplanes and sofas, massive houses with forty-three televisions, even cathedrals don't inspire the inner peace that natural sacraments bring to me. A blueberry makes flowers and berries, for a million years. We make 7-Elevens. Most things we make seem to reduce to smooth surfaces and sharp angles, to keep control of the materials, I guess, but up close, microscopically close, what looks smooth is actually pitted, cavernous, and chaotic. We fashion something that looks grand, but that's the peak of its existence. Inevitably, the moment of creation is the beginning of decay, and the thing will not regenerate itself. A Porsche can only be reborn if a human interferes again. I don't understand how such things can be valued as highly as nature and music and art and literature.

We can help beauty along a bit. We can marry buildings to the landscape, gardens to the climate, clothes to the man—all of that can be pleasing. But the feelings I get on Beech Hill and Bald Rock are different from each other. Beech Nut hut loses luster when I think about how hard we try for permanence and respect and ignore the effortless infinity around us. I think that sod and grasses, however lovely, don't grow naturally on roofs. In contrast, blueberry bushes on a granite ledge don't have to be renovated or re-engineered. Their death and decay contain their own rebirth. Humans are the only beings who can choose to be sterile.

৯৶

In April, I walk the shore and lanes, look through windows, in a state of bursting. The quiet season is coming to an end. I leave the city and come to Maine because of the quiet, and yet, like remembering the Easter Sundays of my youth, disquiet now grows. I can't pretend humans don't exist—there will be lobster boats in the cove and mowers on the lawns, and planes on approach. But nature's noise too will grow. The jazz song of a robin starts at five in the morning. It's building a nest in the shrub right next to the door. A little red squirrel chatters in the spruce, then runs directly up the side of the house for sport. I wish I could live so lightly amid dangers. A moment of goldfinch, a trance of the Allagash is the best I can do to accommodate faith.

I feel summer coming in the bones, in daydreams. Dreaming of summer stretches time out—it seems never to come. Living in summer holds time dear, captive to the chest. Anxiously, I wait: for the machines to start up again and the blueberries to ripen in a season all too short and, in a reverse resurrection, for the time when a man from away can be from here.

Pointed Firs

I'VE ALWAYS BELIEVED that *pointed fir,* like *hairy woodpecker,* was the name of a separate species. Something so iconic deserves to be special, if only to me, for the tree represents all that is compelling about the coast of Maine: the little ones brave and bright-green and still perfectly shaped; the middle-agers rounding into their lovely, conical, and pointed essence with a few missing, wind-downed branches to provide character; and the old ones, grey-green, laconic, many of their branches snapped off in the storms and those that are left drooping with lichen and memories. They look their best right at the edge of a slab of pink granite, often leaning picturesquely for the cameras, pointing at something, before eventually falling at the end of their short lives.

The fir is also associated in my mind with fog, for I've read somewhere that the trees have a special way of thriving in the mist, as if they could hardly live without it.

These two ideas have persisted for years, unexamined, maybe picked up from my periodic reading of *The Country of the Pointed Firs,* and what better time than the third day of a July vacation, fogged-in, to substantiate them?

I wander for a while in the fog of Google. There appears to be no science, no taxonomy behind "pointed," only poetry, for what I get when I search are pages and pages of links to quotes and critics of Sarah Orne Jewett. Of course, I click methodically until I'm completely sure there's nothing new.

Getting rid of "pointed," I gather that these trees framing my view of the bay are balsam firs, since there there's no such thing as a pointed, or maybe they are some kind of spruce. And "fog" and "fir" get me nowhere until I drag in more technical terms, such as "respiration" and (in a derivative flash from high-school biology) "transpiration," which mires me in truly scientific territory, offering links to the abstracts of hundreds of articles, mostly incomprehensible, published in obscure journals.

I glean what I can. In spite of working in scientific publishing nearly my whole working life, my knowledge of trees (indeed the language of science) is pathetic. I'm lost: there's too much information and jargon, and now I doubt everything about my trees. What if the beauties down by the water—barely visible, soupy, spiritual—are indeed spruce, or worse, some kind of common, uninspiring pine? A lifetime of romance is at stake. I might have to give up reading fiction.

Clearly, the thing to do is to leave all this technical stuff for a while and at least distinguish the conifers in my own yard. Okay then, I find a kids' website, All About Trees or some such, and it tells me in plain English that the needles of the fir tree are flat ("you can't roll them in your fingers") and the spruce needles are square-ish ("you can roll them, try it!") and both fir and spruce have needles individually attached to the branch. I walk down the wet grass to the trees and feel for myself. Of course the three at the water's edge are firs. Being always in my view they have to be; they are too perfect in shape to be anything else. Along the side of the yard live the square-ish spruces, a much more utilitarian tree and thankfully so, since their main job is shielding us from the neighbors. I don't bother to look for pines (whose needles apparently attach in groups of two, three, or five). Nor do I get into cones and tree shapes—needles are enough for the ID and one myth is at least partly preserved. To be able to name them pointed would be best, but balsam is okay.

(There was a fleeting Google-glimpse of a balsam = balm = Balm of Gilead connection, but I don't care to get theological right now.)

So what about the fog? (Speaking of theology . . .) Firs and fogs actually get along very well, it turns out. I'm pleased to discover that fog aids trees in at least three ways: there's the way fog condenses on needles and drips to the soil below ("fog drip" seems to be the technical term—really); there's direct absorption through the needles; and finally (more generically true for all trees), fog reduces heat and increases humidity, so when the stomata in the needles (leaves) open up (transpire) to take in carbon dioxide, they don't lose as much oxygen and water in the process. Almost all of the literature I scan concerns research into narrowing stands of old-growth redwoods, or the disturbing fact that acid pollution seems to concentrate in fog. Neither bodes well for the planet, or my fantasy, and the only reference I can find about a true symbiotic relationship is that one species of very rare California conifer that only exists in areas with heavy fog. Well, that's California for you, another one up on the East Coast now that my mythical marriage of fog and fir is discovered to be one of convenience, not true love.

I'm not quite ready to give up. Memorable hours of gazing at the fog-draped firs and rejoicing in their connubial bliss don't die easily. There must be a reference in *The Country of the Pointed Firs*, for it's a relationship both so sensible and spiritual that Mrs. Almira Todd would not fail to remark upon it. I pick up the book and by the time I finish (in two stages: the Maine copy gets me through the end of the vacation and the Massachusetts copy well into the lag time spent in the city before I can get back here to reality), I'm pretty sure, but not entirely, since one gets so easily lost in the world of Dunnet Landing, that neither Jewett nor Todd has anything enlightening to say about firs and fog. This should not be surprising. There's very little fog in the book at all, either physical or linguistic. Time passes and change occurs in the clearest and most serene way possible, not matched in other literature, or life.

What an odd expectation, to read fiction to capture a fact that proves a romance. A tree is made more real when it's connected in time and space to an imagined sea captain's widow dispensing thoroughwort elixir a hundred years ago? But that's exactly what I feel. The pointed fir does not exist in science, and the balsam—in spite of its sappy connotations of Christmas, and (OK, I couldn't help looking it up) Christian cure-alls brewed from fir resin in Palestine—is made more beautiful because of it. What good is knowledge unless it leads to tremulous joy, a Dunnet Landing of one's own?

The firs before me suddenly are enveloped in waves of images—the herbs and haddock of Mrs. Todd, test tubes and pulpits from my past, wife and daughters laughing at the dinner table—and they point to that moment I live for: the emptying hollow in the stomach that travels up to bring mist to the eyes and purpose to the mystified. And then the moment is gone.

Felling Trees

L INCOLN IS THE PROPRIETOR of Link's Lawn Service, a one-and-a-half-man operation in Owls Head. Link does lawns, but his real specialty is trees, or was until he got older. I got to know him a little better after the big southeaster last November. A southeaster is particularly hard on trees, I found out. The wind comes roaring off the bay like a northeaster, but at an unaccustomed angle, and the trees on the shore, the pines and firs, which are used to pushing one way against the north wind, are felled, and their shallow roots that spread against the granite are pulled up like pancakes; in the woods behind the house, the white pines twist, and torque builds, and sometimes a tree just explodes.

I drove up from Boston as soon as I could. The alarmist email from our neighbor Mary said there were "trees down all over the place," and I was panicked that the pointed firs in front, right on the shore, book-perfect in shape, the creatures that define Maine for me, were among the victims. Mary was right and wrong. Our icons had survived, but three others hadn't.

On the south side, the wind uprooted a spruce and leaned it snugly against the white pine just outside our property line. On the north boundary a big fir lay in a thicket of little pines filling a space the last big storm had cleared. In back, across the leaching field, a birch was down. The house was spared, although I saw later that one spruce just yards away had dangerously increased its lean. I left a message on Link's answering machine, and over the next few months, while Link cleared the trees and I traveled between houses, our modest partnership evolved.

Link is the kind of guy who starts talking as soon as he gets into the house. "You should have seen me and Richie working that thicket. Good thing you were down Boston way, you would have laughed at us. But we were crying, believe me, the way that sucker fell, the angles were like to break your back. By the way, you want me to thin those little ones out, I'm happy to. They'll grow better not all tucked up in bed. Anyway, that fir in there was ornery as a mule, even Richie couldn't move the sucker and got mad. And he's a lot younger than me!" Link laughed and paused. "A lot younger. I'm already cutting back on the lawns, we had forty-one, down to twenty or so. I can't do it all anymore, the bad knee locks up. It's just waiting for October when Medicare's going to take care of me."

I said something inane like "Only a few months until the big day, then," but it didn't matter. Not knowing what to say was not a problem when you talked to Link, who was about as opposite a taciturn Mainer as you could get.

"Ay-up. Make me a new man. Sorry I couldn't get out here earlier. The storm was something else, backed us up for months. Well. Best get to work."

That day in May he was finally going to chunk up the birch that had fallen on the leaching field. I had de-limbed it, with a chainsaw borrowed from a friend, but had never used a chainsaw before and didn't dare progress to real cutting. I watched Link hobble up the walkway steps towards his truck. He was without help today, a man grizzled and worn beyond his years, which were only a few more than mine. It was more than hobbling. It was more than a bad knee. His whole body looked crooked. I tried to imagine handling machinery and logs in that kind of pain, and failed. His world was beyond me, but I still felt the raspy grip from his hard hand, cut and thorny like the bark of the trees we loved in our different ways.

Link's son Richie survives in a more protean Maine fashion. He helps his father with the lawns and the trees but he is also a handyman, a carpenter, a musician, a cook at Mimi's Bistro in town. He came over with his father one day and I watched as together they estimated the work and materials needed to replace the walkway steps. They were equals. There seemed no father-son discord, Link calculating and theorizing in a streak of words and Richie comfortably agreeing or amplifying as necessary. I don't know if there had ever been conflict over the metal Richie wore in his eyebrows and ears; if there had been, it was over. I couldn't imagine enough leisure in their hardscrabble lives for the kind of rebellion I inflicted on my own father.

Link could no longer fell the trees himself, but he must have done so in his prime, for in the Maine way he still had the town's tree removal contract, referring the heavy work to Northeast Tree Service. After the birch was chunked up, we decided that the spruce leaning ominously towards the house, the storm's fourth souvenir, had to come down. Two men eventually arrived from Northeast Tree, one a voluble young man in his thirties and the other a very young man, a boy even, in training or just helping out for the day. The felling of the spruce was a brutal and beautiful operation that I watched from the safety of the house: spurs jabbing into the trunk, wide leather belt shinnying up the tree; fierce little chainsaw lopping off all the branches and then toppling the crown as if harvesting a Christmas tree in the sky; long ropes attached to what was left of the top, insurance against a crooked fall; a wedge cut at the base; a fall perfectly placed between garden and house. Then, with a big chainsaw, the master destroyed the tree into six-foot lengths and the apprentice dragged what was left of the tree into cruelly small piles. The massacre took less than an hour and was worthy of every ancient meaning of "fell."

Later, Link would cut the logs into woodstove lengths and chip or haul away the branches. My part in this carbon-cycle symphony would follow, as it has for all the slaughtered trees: wheelbarrow the chunks to the side of the garage and pile them for drying; on a cold fall day or a warm winter one, split the pieces with an axe and stack them in the garage for more drying; in a year or so, burn them to provide warmth, a small strike against energy cartels and the primitive satisfaction of having worked as a body, not a brain.

I was going to ask the tree guys, since they were here anyway, to take down a little dead white pine at the edge of the shore, for them a minute's work with the chainsaw. But I forgot, accidentally on purpose, as my father would say when he felt forgiving, and on a cool day in July, I ventured out with handsaw and axe. It was just a little tree, maybe twenty-five feet tall, four or five inches in diameter, but it struggled against me before succumbing to the dimensions demanded by the woodstove.

Every few minutes I had to stop, to ease my back, wring the cramps out of my hands, wipe away sweat, and gaze out at the beauty of the bay, at the forested islands, and to the north, precious in the imagination, at the ocean of trees in Maine's Great North Woods. Away from the cities, the release of carbon is so obvious, its sequestration so simple. A tree grows to stand among its fellows like a protector and savior. It falls, naturally or not, and its wood yields grudgingly to the saw, giving up its lovely rings of patient years. The splitting axe reveals the fragrant river of fibers inside. Then, in the stove, each log vanishes in an inferno of burned oxygen and freed carbon. I don't understand how atoms can be all this—pure energy in themselves, nothing really but imagination and belief, a god if you will.

The wilderness of the North Woods, reality and inspiration, offers salvation to those of us who have little else to believe. Each step of a tree's life and death should be marked like a holy pilgrimage.

I labored over that dead little tree for two hours. It was surprisingly strong. The inside core of its trunk had only a streak of punk; something else had killed it. Or was it enough to kill, this hint of cancer, this chaotic mush where there once was order? There was no other reason for its death that I could see. It stood in the wind for as long as it could.

As my father had. Like Link, he worked hard, as if to hasten time. Unlike Link, the only physical work he did was a bit of suburban mowing and raking and gardening. The rest of his life was a religious mission. He was a teacher and a principal in a Calvinist Christian school system, following the call of God from school to school, moving us every three or four years to another small town, and it seemed to me that he lived anxiously, always on stage as an arbiter of values and discipline, always performing in front of the school boards he served. Perhaps the yard work was a release, but I never felt him relax in those small towns. His release was summer, which we spent in the woods of northern Michigan, far from the dusty, treeless, judgmental plains. He was a big, soft man, but by August each year he was brown, and had lost some of the weight anxiety had put on him, and his hands were tougher from dirt and rake and raspberry cane, like mine after some sessions with trees. And each September we returned to the fray, both of us, all our working lives. Neither of us could match Link's way of living in the world; when I mentioned to Link one day that there was blood on his hands, he looked at them, at their old cracks and scars, at new cuts, and casually wiped them on his overalls.

My father lived for work, but his work was unrooted, and a fell curse, and he could pass only its sturdiness and none of its salvation to his son. So I cut his doctrine down. Our conversations retreated from rebellions to banalities. And now he is preparing to return to dust, battling the cancer in his core.

Where there had been trees there are now three stumps: from the fir knocked down in the big winds, a few feet of trunk that not even Link and Richie could reduce for burning, its roots still attached where they were ripped out of the thin soil at the very edge of the bank; the straight white cut of spruce, professionally handled close to the ground; the hacked-up stub of my little pine. In consequence the view is opened up a bit, as if affording a clearer vision of Maine's Unorganized Territories to the north, their very name a revelation.

Except that there is still a little tree in the way, exposed now where it was hidden before, a pretty ridiculous-looking thing maybe fifteen feet high, still half-living, species unknown, with only a few scraggly branches left, one of which springs strangely at the top like a cowlick. It's a childish kind of rebellion, I know, that I won't chop it down, but I have come to believe that in the absence of doctrine, and fathers, trees connect the earth to the sky, and only the tree cutter's simple physical grace saves him from sacrilege.

Rockweed

THE ROCKS WE PERCHED ON still show at high tide. The rising sea has not yet taken them—as a refuge, or a memory, they may last our lifetimes. They peek out above the waves like a little archipelago, dry and safe.

When the girls were young, we ventured out almost daily, especially in the first blush of vacation. It was an exercise in re-bonding our fractured suburban lives. We could get to the rocks only at low tide, and we would not stay long, for the tide rises quickly on these shores, and the surf is unpredictable, and it would have been a little too adventurous having to disembark, or embark for that matter, in the wet. No, we climbed up our battlements when the only barrier to access was the slippery rockweed littering our path. The tops of the rocks themselves were weed-free, un-colonized, suitable for timid people from cities south, exciting for two young girls, nine and seven, who liked to pretend they perched on unassailable islands, perfect for their father who knew better but hoped for a different future anyway.

The rockweed presented a problem, though. It looked irredeemably slimy. We stepped around it, in a crooked, almost drunken way, not brave enough to touch by foot and certainly never by hand. "Ewww!" That totem word of childhood afflicted my family too. I even warned my girls when we set off down the shore about less obvious dangers, the barnacles that would scrape your skin raw, and those black or green mold-like patches on the boulders we negotiated. "Don't step there," I said, "especially if it looks wet. It's very slippery." Naturally, then, they were warned off the rockweed, whose piles appeared bottomless and would suck them in—not to test it in our nice sneakers certainly, no matter what live treasures of crab and baby lobster lay all goggle-eyed underneath. In our early pilgrimages we avoided most things organic, which die and rot and stink; our special rocks were dry, clear of processes unknown, safe above the tide.

A few years later we discovered tidal pools. The three of us had been progressing farther and farther away from home, and about a quarter mile down the shore, past the houses on the bluff and a long stretch of jumbled beach, we found classic Maine pink granite ledge, smooth and worry-free. The pools were hidden, flooded at high tide, barely accessible at low. But we persisted, older now, less squeamish, contorting our bodies to peer into crevices where the rewards were hundreds of snails and a score of exotic starfish. I even started combing through the rockweed a bit, lifting it up like great hanks of hair to show the girls the cute little green crabs hiding in the fronds. I didn't know at the time that some of those crabs were invasives from the south, pleased to enter the warming waters of the Gulf of Maine and feast on lobster like the rest of us tourists.

We've progressed far in fifteen years. The world is hotter, and seems more violent, or at least more instantly connectible to disaster. Maine is now more than a refuge for me, now that my daughters are grown and gone, one still on the Atlantic but the wrong side, in Denmark, and the other just moved to California, an hour from the ocean but the wrong one. Maine is an ark. This week after Thanksgiving I sit in the house, staring at water, staring east in fact but both east and west in spirit. The solitude of the shore seems tinged with loneliness today, a place halfway between, and although I give thanks for new lives and exciting independence, I miss my children terribly.

·❧·

Seaweed is the icon of Maine least likely to star on a blog or a bro-chure. If you look closely, you might see a frond peeping out at the base of Thunder Hole in Acadia, or a strand or two on the great expanse of Old Orchard Beach, or a discreet pile artfully arranged around a lobster about to be boiled. The photographer or dreamer operates generally at high tide, when seaweed hides, when the lines between surf and stone are clean. Mess doesn't sell.

But the stuff is everywhere, especially the farther north you go, where the shores wear it thick as an ill-fitting wig, not entirely useless but almost. It is harvested, to be sure, as fertilizer and thickener, and it has achieved a little notoriety as "sea vegetables." The various kelps, for example, have long been eaten around the world (the nori of sushi rolls in Japan, dulse as a cocktail party snack in Ireland), but seaweed is down at the bottom of the roster of marine exploitables. Most Americans like their food familiar, bland, processed by Big Ag; seaweed has a strong taste and smells of low tide even after drying and processing. The number of evangelists for seaweed, even in Maine with its riches, approaches zero.

When all the fish are gone, perhaps only then we'll turn to Gouldsboro Bay, where a seventy-year-old man, probably crazy by modern definitions, cuts kelp by hand, standing in a wetsuit on offshore ledges, buffeted by heavy surf. We'll believe him when he praises kelp's effect on his immune system, and we too will pray for the enlightenment of humankind: eat kelp, live long, for it will restore the seawaters whence we came and heal our guts and blood. We'll believe the research and the analysis, the richness of kelp's minerals, trace elements, vitamins, enzymes, high-quality proteins, and the ever-sexy phytochemicals, the claims of tumor inhibition and reduction of cholesterol and conquering of viruses. But not until we're desperate, in the coming dystopia.

Rockweed, however, the most plentiful seaweed, is not very edible, not even by New Age humans, and has been harvested but minimally for fertilizers, advertising no sex appeal whatsoever. Until recently.

It's one thing to see a man in a skiff scraping rockweed off ledges with a long-handled rake. It's quite another to see a huge mechanical harvester in your cove. In the new age of peak oil, natural fertilizers look pretty good after all.

Rockweed dominates the intertidal zone of many northern shores. It grows slowly; after a normal life span of ten to fifteen years, its fronds may have reached eight feet long. It survives all but the heaviest of surfs by attaching to rock with sucker-like holdfasts. It sports air-filled bladders along the fronds, to lift it to sunlight at high tide. Scientists say that as many as one hundred fifty species of animals—birds and shellfish and minnows hiding out—rely on rockweed for survival. Thus, Maine's fishing industry may depend on it. And rockweed protects not only commerce, but the whole shore. Not for nothing is it commonly called knotted wrack, as if to cushion the intertidal zone from the ruin of ocean storms.

I wish that, at the beginning of my years here, those very years while my daughters were growing into their own lights, I had focused us more, found one baby rockweed plant, say, marked its holdfast, and every week crouched at the shore, in the wet, in our old sneakers, to observe its progress to adulthood. That bit of shore would have become precious in an entirely different way.

Stepping back now from that edge, I can at least suggest that "knotted wrack" is a wonderful description of our current dilemmas.

Predictably, every living thing, even weeds, will be exploited eventually. Predictably, environmentalists find a bully pulpit only when the big machines arrive. It's inevitable that the Rockweed Coalition ("no-cut zones") will battle the Maine Seaweed Council ("the sustainable use of seaweed"). Our ecological problems are as local as ownership of the intertidal zone in Maine (nobody quite knows who can do what, the law is ancient and not clear); as knotty as livelihoods versus legacies; as intractable as feeding the stomachs and aspirations of seven billion people.

A few years ago in our cove, we could expect to see a moored boat or two almost every summer day. Rakers scoured the sea bottom for sea urchins to satisfy the craze in Japan, and in two years the urchins were wiped out. This past summer the price of elvers, baby eels highly prized in Asia, reached $2,000 a pound. I give the fishery maybe five years before it's gone. An invasive red seaweed from Asia via Europe threatens our New England shores; it suffocates all life in its path, stinks when it dies, and ironically enough, might be controlled by sea urchins. Every day of every year, the US loses 5,000 acres of land to development. I listen to my daughters talk about climate change. There's despair in their voices, a resignation to the inevitable.

The idyll in Maine may last longer than in most places, but we lucky ones have equipped only ourselves to survive, have equipped no descendants to adapt, and we survive mostly by dreaming, sitting on our rocks above the tides.

⌇

Rachel Carson, in *The Edge of the Sea*, called it the underwater forest: "The trees of the forest are the large sea weeds, known as rockweed, or sea wracks, stout of form and rubbery of texture. Here all other life exists within their shelter—a shelter so hospitable to small things needing protection from drying air, from rain, and from the surge of the running tides and the waves, that the life of these shores is incredibly abundant."

"Small things": the plainness of prose can sometimes be devastating. The shore still calls out thrillingly, here in Maine especially, but Carson's simple joy from just sixty years ago echoes today with the terrible probability of its loss. Even the simplest shore will be stripped. I look at it as if some kind of sympathetic pain, some horrible probe from the future, is invading our days and fracturing our DNA and our children's DNA, leaving but a moment or two, here and there, of fullness.

We know we're failing the forests, yet we continue on raking, year by inevitable year. Which means that the human essence is now failing, which means that I too am failing to protect these smallest of things, a minnow, or a weed, or a girl's touch. It's so easy to sit by, stunned and timid, just because I can still find a primeval sense of life in Maine, because Maine can offer to my family and to anybody who believes in these words some kind of sanctuary, the way life used to be, a place where blood is still seawater. I respond to the seashore too often just for its beauty, or in fear of its slime, and do little about its exploitation besides manipulate words. And if that's the legacy I've given my daughters . . . well, I haven't shown them how to muck, how to see like an animal. We've gotten far too used to our lavish city comforts, to our ability to escape in our cars from the cars.

The very nature of our bodies is being altered—that essence of salt water in our veins, those proteins in our brains designed over millions of years to treasure sunshine and open space and the creatures, even the slimiest, of the shore. I wish now that I had taken the girls squishing and laughing into the forest. I wish we had gone a little crazy in the surf. It might have made these passages a little easier.

Beyond Ash Point

THE TURN-AROUND AT ASH POINT is built up of junk. To get to the water, you have to clamber down a pile of bulldozed and broken concrete blocks, some state bureaucrat or out-of-town landowner's idea of progress, an ugly man-made mess if not for the beach roses and Muscle Ridge Islands growing all around. A few tourists do come, to park and drag kayaks down the slope, or to take a couple of minutes to enjoy the view before returning to the map and the road and the next peninsula. It is a lovely and pristine view, elevated by the concrete, looking out on the bay, as long as you ignore the ranch house to the right, and the forlorn rusty utility pole and streetlight next to you, and on the left the large, plain Victorian farmhouse grandly announcing itself, in three-foot letters, "Trails End." Once on the shore, I don't look back.

Assuming time and solitude enough, I have two shore routes from which to choose the way back home: the direct route to the south, along the conservation land, or the walk out to Lucia Beach, and then home along the road. The third route, simply fast-walking back up the hill and retracing my steps, is for guilty days with kids and schedules and those little responsibilities that vacation brings.

Until the past year, I always took the south route. For most of the way, it is an archetypal Maine coast of granite ledges, fir trees, and surf. The ospreys we see fishing in front of our house fly down this way with their catches and must have their nest in these woods. I imagine deer (bear? moose? puma? saber-toothed tiger? why not?)

walking along the trails at the edge of the bluff and venturing down now and then to drink from the pools of rainwater on the ledge. Coming from home, the kids and I discovered gorgeous tidal pools a few years ago, full of snails and crabs and pink starfish we counted and named. There's a bit of danger too, appropriate for these several hundred acres of land in trust that give the illusion of wilderness; you really should plan this walk for low tide, for high tide forces you up on steep boulders and ledges to get across some deep crevices, and you cling to bushes and dead trees to pass, or, feeling old, give up and climb up farther and walk the deer trails for a while. Back on the shore, when the conservation land stops and the houses begin, you can't really see them. They are hidden by the bluff. And there's nothing like climbing the rocks at the end and coming out on your own front lawn to give you a sense of satisfaction.

But lately it's the shoreline to Lucia Beach that draws me. Perhaps I've been less settled, perhaps I need a little more drama in my recreation.

The incredible gamut of stone on this half-mile of shore is one obvious attraction. Rocks large and small and gravelly, granite ledges in slabs and tongues, a sand beach rare in our neck of the woods test ankles and invite poetry. I stop and marvel every few yards.

In contrast to the dramatic changes of stone, the views seaward change subtly. As Ash Island recedes behind me, I look at the islands lying on the bay edge of Muscle Ridge Channel. (Some maps name it Mussel Ridge—no poetry there.) They have names—Hurricane, Garden, High, Flag, Clam Ledges, Otter—but none looks inhabited, just intriguing, glowing, ephemeral, and as you stumble along they grow and fade on the horizon like clouds, like muscles flexing. I'm not particularly an island lover—they are too easily spoiled by money or people essentially mad—but that these are mansion-less makes me glad. Those of us who are land-bound still need the illusion of escape; our houses and ocean-side gardens could still be invaded.

Just before Lucia Beach, indeed partly overlooking it—just before the two ranch houses, a three-story condo affair, and their suburban lawns slightly assault the senses—sits a small, eccentric, perfect house:

gray, crooked, rooms like ship cabins, set among firs on ledge, a score of windows gazing on surf and sand. Is envy the real reason I walk to Lucia Beach?

Today it's something else. Today is Thursday, the sixteenth of October, a work day for most of America. Not for me. I was fired last month. I come up from a crevice in the ledge, a small thunder hole where I have stood for a while, listening to the waves groan, and see what I'm always alert for. There's movement at the top of the bank, just at the edge of the bushes. Some small dark animal, so brown as to be nearly black, ventures out and immediately ducks into safety on seeing the human. Just an otter, I think, rare enough at the ocean's edge. But it's too black, maybe it's a mink. Whatever it is, it's rare and wild and it lives among us—wary of our dogs and development, not so casual as the deer and osprey, but here. And I have to sit down. All of it together—the islands, the surf, the fir trees, the mink—bring tears to my eyes, tears of elation and longing and desperate worry about it all being taken away.

And that's why we obsess about houses on the waterfront. Turn your back on your troubles. You have arrived. You can afford this, you should have no worries. Look out in front of you, it's the illimitable ocean, you're safe, they can't get you here.

But of course they can, and I walk humbled past the Perfect House. There's a new hot tub on the lawn. My life's been changed for corporate reasons. We are capable of beauty, seeing it and making it and losing it, and on this sparkling day, in my second week of unemployment, I touch one foot to the sand, just to make a mark before the tide comes in, then climb up the rocks to Lucia Beach Road and the way home, grateful at least for this moment in time.

Yellow Finches

THE FRAME I HAVE ON PENOBSCOT BAY is about twenty feet wide. This is the unobstructed view; blue water (or green or gray or silver, depending on the sky) does peek through the outstretched branches of the pointed firs that form the right and left boundaries of my collector's box. The bottom of the box comprises Adirondack chairs on the lawn, the top sun and moon and lightning and stars. Across the frame, from fir to fir, flit little yellow jewels.

I can observe worlds through my frame: the tides covering and uncovering the seaweed on Little Island; dragonflies and hatches of flying ants; gulls, elegant terns, osprey, crows, loons, cormorants, eider ducks; small red squirrels that chatter in the branches before dashing across the opening, and once in a great while Brer Fox making his rounds along the ledge; the neatly nibbled stems of phlox shortened overnight, hinting of deer; lobster traps moving closer to shore as the summer progresses; people in boats and airplanes, working and pleasure, the occasional tourists in yellow kayaks. Among these many wonders, today I think about the finches.

At least I'm assuming they are finches. I look them up in *Sibley*. None of the regular finches are yellow, but there are three goldfinches—Lawrence's, Lesser, and American. There's also a page of exotic finches that regularly escape from captivity and occasionally compete successfully enough to form feral colonies. I don't have a sharp image in my head of what bird I've glimpsed, so I page through the whole book, looking for more yellow. There are orioles, tanagers, and grosbeaks, but they are bigger, eight inches in length. Warblers occupy pages and pages, all yellow, all around five inches, many in the right territory. Well, OK, I'm not sure I'm up for this confusion of birds, this riot of evolution, so I'm putting my money on the American goldfinch, which will require a closer and longer look. I've seen the little guys fly back and forth, low along our small cliff as if they have nests down there, and I think I need to be at the cliff's edge for the best view. Which lets me in for the temptation of the wider view.

This is what scientists strive to ignore while they work: I walk from the deck down to the water and can now see the ends of Sheep and Monroe Islands, and the low, blue seductive curves of Vinalhaven, and the open ocean to the southeast (all the way to Spain if my orientation is correct). But I must focus on a tiny area even while accepting these stereoscopic glories circling around. I have to look for a little yellow speck, and now I'm nearly in its flight path, and will it show itself at all?

I resolve to spend an hour, concentrating. The sounds of the surf and the lobster boats make it hard to distinguish bird song, and I swivel around even at a robin's screech. I scan the tall trees behind, the short bushes on the shore. At the half hour there's a brief glimpse of what might be a female finch, but the brief comedy of taking off eyeglasses and putting on binoculars misses the ID. I wait some more, getting distracted by guys laying a new string of lobster traps, thinking that science has become magical. If I had wireless, I could pluck that American goldfinch right out of the air and make all of its data and songs and closely related species appear on my screen. (Could do that back in the house, too, through the wire, which illusion seems more understandable than what happens in the ceaseless surf of electromagnetic wave theory.) Does this disconnect between pixels and reality explain my slight sense of anxiety, wanting the real thing to appear, wanting to know something solid, scientific, historical about the marvelous place I inhabit?

No small yellow thing appears. I'm in the frame, I must be interfering with the observation.

Charles Darwin made some of his most dramatic discoveries in finches. He didn't really know it at the time—he brought back a dead dozen specimens from the Galapagos Archipelago, presented them to the Geological Society of London on January 4, 1837 along with a lot of other stuff, and left the corpses for others to classify. The birds weren't even named after him until a hundred years later. But of course he realized what he had seen in the perfect gradation in the size of their beaks. In the book that eventually became *The Voyage of the Beagle,* he wrote, "Seeing this gradation and diversity of structure in one small, intimately related group of birds, one might really fancy that from an original paucity of birds in this archipelago, one species had been taken and modified for different ends." (Note the passive voice—he wasn't quite able to proclaim that God is dead.) In the course of a couple of million years, a finch that migrated from Central or South America evolved into fourteen species with dramatically different ways of coping with changing climatic conditions. One now feeds on ticks plucked from tortoises and iguanas, one scrapes at dead tree branches to eat larvae, several eat seeds like finches around the world, and one—the vampire—tears at the feathers of red-faced boobies to drink their blood.

And what will happen to those small, harmless, non-descript birds in our new world? One species is already nearly extinct from fishermen tearing up their mangrove habitat in search of sea cucumbers, and the others are threatened with new, dramatic, un-climatic conditions of cats, rats, and parasitic flies.

Darwin's expedition left England on December 27, 1831 and returned October 2, 1836. He had the widest view of nearly any human of his time, and the narrowest. He killed nature in order to study it. He spent countless hours, even years, in close observation and communion. Our folks get impatient with time passing and want the Internet to tell them their circumstances.

I return to the house for lunch and some surfing.

The next day, sitting on the deck away from the ledge, chastely uninvolved with its "bounding flight and distinctive flight calls," I make the identification of the American Goldfinch almost immediately.

Obligingly, a male proudly perches high up and far out on a branch of the fir tree to the right (and defecates), and a few minutes later a female grooms herself briefly inside the fir to the left. The male is bright yellow, with a black forehead and wings. The female is paler, without that rakish black hat. They are both very plump, fatter than Sibley shows—life on the shore must be rewarding for birds as well.

Like every species in the world, however common and wide-spread, the goldfinch is unique. They line their nests with thistle-down, so tightly woven that sometimes a rain storm will accumulate enough water to drown the chicks. They are mostly monogamous, usually gregarious, and ubiquitous. They are the only finch to molt completely, they migrate just far enough to stay reasonably warm, and they have thrived in the presence of human deforestation. It is a thoroughly sensible species.

I feel excellent having made its acquaintance. I'm in the process of adapting city ways to country life, and welcome the chance to believe that the more our lives become virtual, the more we seek the tangible; the more that news, usually concerning a disaster or a war, becomes instantly available anywhere in the world, the less it means. Suffering is de-personified. Is this why almost no one talks about nuclear war anymore?

Maybe things aren't quite as bleak as in 1960, when John Steinbeck, traveling across the Mojave with Charley, wrote, "Even our own misguided species might re-emerge from the desert. The lone man and his sun-toughened wife who cling to the shade in an unfruitful and uncoveted place might, with their brothers in arms— the coyote, the jackrabbit, the horned toad, the rattlesnake, together with a host of armored insects—these trained and tested fragments of life might well be the last hope of life against non-life." The Cold War has evolved into a series of religious wars; somehow these seem more tractable than nukes if only the combatants would examine the power of life in the sub soils of their deserts and the shores of their voyages.

Almost Heaven

You've made the trip to and from DC scores of times. It was bad enough on the shuttle, with the lawyers and the politicos taking up all the oxygen. But these days discomfort replaces distaste, for the airlines that trapped you in their frequent flyer programs have taken to flying BOS-DCA in soft little jets, euphemistically called "regional," in which you go outside to board, stoop to walk the aisle, and add to the calluses on your knees just by sitting. And they fly lower, in more turbulence, and today, especially today, your hold on life seems a little shakier: you wish you were a lawyer, in certainty of something, but you've been trained in eschatology, not tautology, and your mind reverts more than usual to the various ways of achieving salvation.

Naturally, heaven with a capital "H" jumps in first, and you sit there, flying through the saucy clouds in a tube of pasta, considering the possibilities.

In the Protestant world, if the plane could only climb just a few light years higher into pure eternity, closer to . . . well, that's the way your relatives would urge you to think. You think it's more likely that the plane will crash. Well then, hallelujah! You'll be well-placed to be saved, theoretically at least, what with the predestination gruel you got in your Gerber's, but only if you work fast and repent of your forty-five years of unbelief before hitting the ground. Your mother always hoped you would (repent, that is, not crash) (although it's hard to get on your knees in a Bombardier).

On tipsy transatlantic flights Buddhism occasionally tempts. Reincarnation of flesh makes sense from the point of view of indestructible atoms, and Nirvana has the ineffable appeal of being entirely opposite of Heaven—no apocalypse, you can do it if you try, nothing and everything is real, paradise lives on earth.

Islam does not tempt, not even when you're stuck on the tarmac waiting out the terror of a storm cell. Its vision of Paradise is entirely too graphic (women, water, wine, wealth), so where's the intrigue in that?

You fly out of the turbulence just off New York. For one last time you think of the dreadful presentation you experienced just a few hours ago in DC, the nasty clients, how you haven't lost the ability to grin obsequiously in front of gritted teeth. But that's behind you and below you, and you relax a little, you're on the way home, and you've trained yourself over the years to indulge in the real fantasy, heaven with the small "h":

The dream of retirement, that's what sustained you through all the years of business travel—flying Boston-LA for a one-hour meeting, countless presentations in featureless hotels, cities awash in franchises, foreign countries foggy from jet lag, mercurial bosses—and all the years in an office (Robert Frost: "The brain is a wonderful organ. It starts working the moment you get up in the morning and does not stop until you get into the office."). Heaven was spelled M-a-i-n-e. You had vacation tastes of it for twenty-five years: a camp on a lake, and then a house on the ocean. By the end of your office days, you were desperate for air and trees and unfettered time to think and write. You retired early. Except that the company asked you to stay on part-time for a while, and now you exist in limbo: half in proposals, half in freedom; still suspended between air and earth.

Your one-year anniversary of retirement approaches and you still haven't figured heaven out even though you now get to live there half the time. Maybe it's because you left a steady income at the same time the market bubbles burst. What's your worth as a man if every day the numbers are red? At least you haven't fallen down dead from a heart attack, bored and discombobulated outside the comforting tracks of the work-a-day world. You've got plenty to occupy your time, in this fumbling about for future happiness.

What exactly is the future? On days such as today, it's like a dose of oxytocin, giving birth to all sorts of fanciful rural ideas, and then, blissfully, helping you un-remember the kid behind you kicking the seatback, your aching hips and tender knees, the cost of those frequent flyer miles. You just fly away to another state of mind, where the office abuts Penobscot Bay. You slide from your airplane seat to the Adirondack chair down by the shore, where you get the water in the eye and the ecstasy in the muscles of which Buddha and St. Peter boast, there's that second or two of melting into nature as the luminescent future spans the Bay, and then, abruptly, it stops coming at you. A commuter jet, delighting in its approach to Knox County Regional just beyond the shore, blasts through the early summer air just above and makes you an ironic present of the present. OK, you think, yanked back to the Bombardier, the future never comes. Love the gifts you are given. Forget fantasies and investments. Deal with the surly prospects, the large dogs menacing your poodle on her daily walks, the large oil bills menacing your desk, the moss on your Maine lawn creeping northward and the dandelions creeping southward, and the gray filling your beard. You will soon alight. The moment of the roaring engine's absence will be long and sweet.

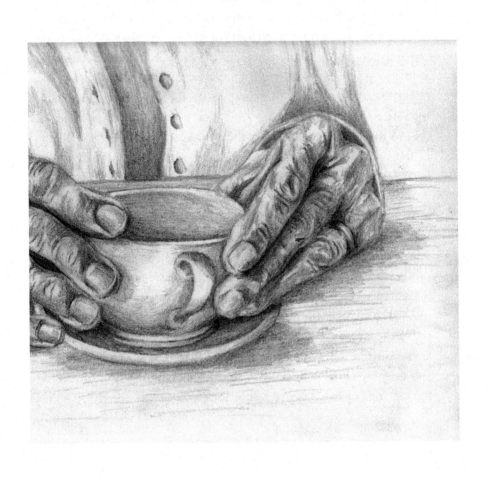

Maine Mundane

The rounds you make on a Tuesday or Wednesday morning are simple. First, the dump: you slide the minivan's third seat forward, making room for the garbage, the old stained boxes for recycling metal and glass, the several bags of returnables; you drive down Dublin Road past the airport and through South Thomaston and over to Buttermilk Lane and the Waste Transfer Station, the ugliest acre of land in the county; you start breathing through your mouth; you wait your turn behind the guys in pickups. The man in the little shed (Waste Operations Manager?) pops out and says, "Hi, up from the city for a while now?" and you talk to him because he's also from Massachusetts.

Second, the Redemption Center: the guy here has never said a word to you in several years of returning bottles; you wait as he expertly tosses Poland Spring and Squirt and the various products of cola conglomerates into tall cardboard boxes; you look at the hundreds of beer bottles displayed on shelves running around the low room; you wonder if it means he's pathologic if he doesn't even acknowledge your thank-you for the $3.50, less seventy-five cents for the local paper, that he lays in your hand.

Third, the South End Grocery: you stop here because there's always something you're missing on vacation—milk, soda, chips; you can never easily find what you want in its hot aisles crowded with plastic-wrapped prepared foods; you usually avoid buying a big-city paper out of principle, but sometimes you just can't help gloating how hot it must be in Boston and you give in to the *Globe*.

Occasionally you extend these forty-five minutes of chores with a ten-minute detour around the perimeter of Owls Head, in spite of its nearly complete lack of ocean views.

Other days you more or less gladly mow the lawn (and even clip around the stones of the back garden and the ocean garden and the lattice-work of the deck), you sweep the garage and the steps, you mulch the gardens. All the while you aren't thinking of anything profound. In fact, it's likely you aren't thinking at all. The satisfaction you get from mundane things beggars description. Maybe you shouldn't try.

But of course, back home, you can't stop yourself thinking about not thinking. The mundane becomes mythical, takes on Thoreauvian wonder, i.e., what are you escaping? And why not wonder: your work-a-day life consists of obsessive worrying and planning, making progress with the nice automobiles and that soft recliner sliding into The Sopranos, and you can't not think now, there are too many bills to pay. You love to clip grass in Maine knowing you don't have to do it for a living.

Yet you're a Pilgrim driven along another road. The lure of the simple life is your Burden. You want to be rich, how light and easy life would be.

Then you'd have ulcers, and they'd be incurable.

Tea Bags from Shaws

T HE HABIT STARTED IN MAINE, the tea drinking, I mean.
Massachusetts, where I live mostly, is more of a coffee kind of
place—busy lives, kids, jobs. But on a wintry Saturday afternoon in Owls Head, when I'm alone in the house and writing, or
supposed to be writing, the act of sitting with a cup of tea in the rock-
ing chair next to the wood stove is a cultural imperative. The Dutch
have a word for it, *gezellig*, which describes a complex state of warmth
and intimacy and friendliness and belonging that has no English
equivalent.

I worked for a British company for many years and that should
have done the trick with the tea (or maybe that's exactly why it didn't
do the trick—it was not a pleasant company). During that time I
drank tea occasionally: the obligatory "cuppa" during afternoon
breaks in Oxford; while playing Scrabble with my mother; infre-
quently in Maine. Now that I'm working for a Dutch company and
life is more leisurely and predictable, tea has equaled coffee in quantity, and will quite surpass it once I retire. Not in quality, however: I
drink Starbucks from the bean, Shaws brand from the bag. Clearly, tea
is a state of mind.

It reminds me strongly of my grandmother. The tea bag was made
for frugal people like her (for loose leaves must be difficult to re-use).
The tea bag was invented around the turn of the twentieth century,
the same time that Effie arrived from the Netherlands; a New York
merchant named Thomas Sullivan inadvertently commercialized it

when his customers realized they could easily brew a pot or a cup by pouring hot water over the little muslin bags he used for tea samples. Thomas Lipton then came over from London a few years later and gave the tea bag the full American marketing Monty. This all seems to fit: Britain and Holland; ambition; efficient thriftiness.

I think about my grandma as I contemplate retiring (she never really retired). Famously, she saved her tea bags from day to day. I teased her about it, of course, being from a joshing kind of family on both sides, hers and my father's, but it was circumspect and never went so far as to count the times of their re-use. She kept them in a little yellow covered cup next to the stove, and she must have had a rotating disposal system because there were never more than two or three bags in it at a time. In the afternoons, if I didn't have a late class or wasn't due for a shift at the hospital, she'd make me a cup, always a fresh bag for me, or a pot for the both of us. I don't remember if she saved those bags or not (she must have); worse, I don't remember our conversations.

Effie was, I guess, about seventy years old in 1969. I was nineteen, with a certain self-centeredness that went with the times, and knew little about hers, except that she crossed the Atlantic at a very young age, without her parents, who had died. She didn't dwell in the past at all. It was much later when I heard the stories from my mother of Minnesota farm life during the Great Depression, and the death of the grandfather I never met, and Effie's move to Grand Rapids, Michigan with the money from the farm sale and all her children with her except Neal who had escaped to the University of Chicago. Effie kept body and soul together during the war and afterwards by buying a large old house and boarding students from Calvin College in the several bedrooms upstairs. By the time I became one of those boarders the upstairs rooms had been turned into a separate apartment, so I slept in a tiny room off the kitchen for the first half of my sophomore year, and then, when my bachelor uncle Henry at last succumbed to his devils and was remanded to the straitjackets of Pine Rest Christian Home, in his larger room at the front of the house. I was not overly embarrassed by living with my grandma in the year of the Chicago 7.

Reason and parsimony swayed me even then: I had disliked freshman dorm life at Calvin College; sophomores could live off campus with a family member; 1056 Bates Street was near my job at the hospital; the money I paid Grandma was considerably less than the cost of room and board in Vanderwerp Hall. Besides, she allowed me considerable freedom with late nights and odd hours, so much more than parents, in loco or otherwise, would ever have done. That's why I didn't dare to tease her too much about the tea bags. I didn't want to see what she must have been underneath, a hard woman, tight with money, morally demanding, a devil to those of her children who would not believe in God. I just wanted her to be my grandma. And she was. Fortunately for me, her loving and generous spirit skipped a generation and any discussions we had about politics or religion must have been gentle. The trials that were her lot in America made her strict with her children, not me.

I saw the steel at the very end. It seems that she suffered silently with stomach cancer long before she told anyone. I came back to Grand Rapids for a few days before going off to Peace Corps; she had refused hospital care and lay shrunken and rigid in her bedroom off the dining room when I visited. I don't think she even recognized me. She was too busy preparing to meet her Maker.

I received the news two weeks later in Cheongju, South Korea. My mother wrote in one of those blue, fold-over aerograms of the seventies that Grandma had died three days after I left the country.

I knew I would never see her again when I left her bedroom in 1975, and I was guilty for a while and saved the aerogram until its flimsy paper fell apart. But she would have wanted me to go, to start my own trials, to grow up.

I wonder now what she would think about the person I became. She probably wouldn't tell me in any case, but I hope she would at least nod silently when I microwave my cup of tea rather than light a slow and costly burner to heat a full and wasteful kettle.

How to _____ a _____
Lobster _____

A T SOME POINT IN YOUR LIFE, you'll want to believe the writers and the artists, the travel sites and the brochures, and visit the State of Maine. You'll particularly surrender to the coast, we predict, and therefore must try some lobsters. Prepare first for your vacation by watching all possible footage of Acadia's surf and Aroostook's moose and the spectacular loneliness of the Appalachian Trail. (Warning: you'll want to get on the road immediately.) Then, more practically, make sure to view the various "How-to" lobster videos that are out there. You're going to encounter lobster icons everywhere in Maine—they are as numerous as the illusions you are in the market for—and you need to understand that the state employs for its way of life no better scam artist than the lobster: so lowly, so ugly, so busy goosing humans to pretend they're outdoorsy, rugged, independent, rich, sated, pure, primitive, or at least not office-bound; such a fresh and perfect vehicle for carrying dreams, not to mention butter. In fact, lobsters are so good at their job that you'll need help in interpreting the fantasies they raise, help from people like us, who have already succumbed more or less completely to the lure.

Fill in the First Blank

Realize first that lobsters are hardly all about eating. A world of wonder surrounds them.

1. "How to **catch**." In this illusion be prepared to be male and burly and wear a hoodie. Be immune to seasickness; the ocean always seems to be rough on film and you'll pitch around the boat picturesquely. Water splashes over the gunwales, the horizon rises and drops like the water in a toilet tank, the deck is slippery with guts and kelp. It'll be cold, too—wear slickers and gloves. If you're lucky, the lobsters will practically jump out of the traps and into your heart. If not, you can utter stoical comments about next time. This is a boy's dream: out in the wild, in the company of men, reaping from nature where he didn't sow. Even in those videos, the mystique is palpable. You can almost smell the unwashed jeans and the briny air and the rotten herring in the bait bags, feel the saltwater seeping down your neck.

Or, make it slightly more real and arrange to visit our living rooms when you come to Maine. In our little corner of the coast, you can get out the binoculars in comfort and watch our neighbor's son fish in the cove, one man against the elements, so adroit the way he slews the steering wheel around. In effect, the boat drives itself in a nice contained arc as he handles the winch and empties the traps and ties on the bait bags and slides the traps back into the waves. It's not dramatic like the video close-ups of menacing claws but it's pretty nice. The sight makes you feel good—real food, real men just outside your door, everything there for the picking, the perfect sustainable harvest. You can almost imagine the way it used to be when lobsters were so plentiful that kids scooped up basketfuls from the shore, so common that lobsters were contemptible, food for servants, fertilizer for fields. Before the shore was bought up by people from away.

Now this beast is another kind of fodder, for tourists and Mainer wannabes. Lobsters are plentiful (one hundred million pounds landed in Maine last year), about the only creature in the sea that is these days, and therefore you'd think they'd be cheap—which they are considering what the fishermen get at the dock. But then the long chain of distributors and wholesalers and retailers and chefs takes over, adding so much cost that you, having "caught" your dinner in the lobster shack by pointing to it in the tank and then strapping on your plastic bib, will feel privileged just looking at the prices.

Being this kind of tourist is fine, but we encourage you to feel more authentic and mystical and Mainiacal. Rent a house for your vacation, and on at least one evening go to the local fish shop and pick up a bagful of lobsters. Feel even more authentic and wander down to the local town dock and buy from the wholesaler, or better yet, ask our neighbor's son for a few fresh ones off the boat. That's a good story for the folks back home and will be topped off perfectly when you hire Captain Jack to take your family and your Canon out in Rockland Harbor. He'll show you the real thing, in under an hour. Your kids can touch one.

2. "How to **kill**." If you choose the direct route, not the restaurant route, of course you will realize from the commotion in the bag you're carrying that lobsters need to be kept alive as long as possible for best flavor. This means murder in your kitchen. To prepare, watch the lobster scene in "Annie Hall" and practice speaking shellfish—that is, take a light touch, laugh at your lover's squeamishness, and don't forget to take pictures. Above all, don't panic once you're in killing position. (At this point, your modern class of chef-instructor on video politely advises that the timid will want to look away. Julia Child, you'll note if you look her up, didn't bother with such niceties.) The positions are advised to be several. You can grasp your dinner and plunge it head-first into boiling water, or stab with a pick what passes for its brain, or slice down its spinal cord with a sharp knife. However you kill, feel proud that you've at least approached your food supply so closely as to respect it.

3. "How to **cook**." First of all, don't ask what difference it makes whether you boil or steam. We don't have a clue. (Other methods such as grilling or broiling are chosen, we believe, by hosts and chefs who have run out of other ways to impress their guests.) The main point is

to achieve that pretty red color that looks so good on brochures (next to an ear of corn and a pot of butter and a tub of slaw, on a weathered picnic table next to a dock, on a quaint harbor full of boats, at sunset). Do pay a little attention to cooking times, however, unless you enjoy spending seventy-five dollars on the equivalent of old shoes.

4. "How to **eat.**" At last you're really ready to start feeling like something you're not. Rich and sophisticated, perhaps. Or for a different kind of human, earthy. But first you have to dismember the animal. (Do not, we say, if you value your personhood, ever succumb to eating lobster meat pre-split, processed, picked, whatever, except of course on a roll at Red's Eats.) It's fine to go ahead and get your sea legs and first watch those elegant displays on YouTube, the twisting and cracking and picking, the impeccable hand-eye coordination, not a drop of water spilled, not a morsel un-excavated. Not even the spindly legs escape the quest for meat. Just know that the actual creature is awfully messy. Yet do not wear one of those plastic bibs (or if you must, do not so obviously read steps one through seven printed thereon), especially if you're in a restaurant, especially if it's a Maine restaurant. We will shun you. Proper technique will keep your shirt and soul clean.

Try a soft-shell shedder if you're dainty, but understand that real Mainers go for hard-shell. You are certainly permitted to use nut-crackers on the claws and knuckles, but for maximum eew-factor, do not use nutcrackers, and definitely not tin snips, to open up the tail meat. Get in there and use your hands, thusly: after you twist the tail from the body, bend it back near the end and into the resulting crack insert a finger—you choose which one—and push the meat out. Look around and hope someone saw your proctological prow-ess. Feel cool and rustic.

If you have been fortunate enough to rent a house in Maine, or even buy one, and want to cook and eat your own lobsters, here is what not to do: very soon after this instructor and his wife bought their Maine house, we had overnight guests from the city. Lobster of course was called for. Like true Mainerbees, we asked our neighbor, who fished a few pots, if he could spare a half-dozen bugs for dinner (so cool we knew the lingo, so awesome that our food could come right out of our cove!). So far so good, but that was the high point: none of us really knew how to eat a lobster, the claw crackers didn't work, our four collective pre-teen daughters were pretty much stunned with grossness, water seemed to drain endlessly from the shells (and permanently stained the walnut wood of the table, we discovered later), the smell lasted three days because we didn't put out the garbage immediately, and we have not cooked lobster since. So much for mystique: just because one ate lobster doesn't mean one had a Maine experience. If you practice your techniques, however, you may preserve or even enhance your fantasies, especially if you decide to eat that gray-green tomalley stuff inside the body (maximum eew-factor, maximum points) and it isn't quite what you expected.

Finally, if you're richer in money than in imagination, order up a lobster bake, complete with chowder and clams and mussels and slaw and corn and blueberry pie, from some outfit in Bar Harbor, either for inside consumption at one restaurant where (we quote) "you and your guests can watch and take pictures," or for outside authenticity in a fire pit on a beach, on, say, the gala Thursday night of your week on a windjammer.

Fill in the Second Blank

There is really only one word you can employ in this blank. Oh, you might experiment with "rock" (the B-52s singing "Rock Lobster") or "spiny" (but you discover these are crustaceans without claws—impossible), or "langostino" (otherwise known as "squat" and which is really a crab and a made-up restaurant word and beneath contempt). But truly only one word suffices: **Maine**. Take it from us: that search result is two nouns inseparably joined at the hype. Someone at a gathering in Massachusetts will ask us about plans for vacation, and we'll say, "We have a second house in Maine," whereupon the rejoinders will almost always be one question, "On the water?" and two statements, "Pretty cold up there in the winter," and "You must eat a lot of lobster." The simplest response is to say yes to all three.

This reinforces the idea of Maine as Vacationland and dreamscape and a place that most Americans would be terribly bored to stay in for longer than a week or two, which is just how we'd like flatlanders to view it. Bring your money, folks, but do not stay long. Unless, of course, you fully embrace the place. As we are trying so hard to do.

In any conversation about Maine, we do not say how much we are in love with the state, how we wish we could live here permanently; such emotional statements tend to fall flat and no rejoinder or joke will be possible, thus inhibiting the party atmosphere. We do not admit that we really don't care for lobster. It may cause our listeners to combust. We could, however, discuss the lobster's economic importance to the state, and how fishermen are taking affairs into their own hands and certifying Maine lobster against Canadian imports, and we even could mention, depending on the politics and the enthusiasm of the circle around us, one of two ideas: with Republicans, Linda Bean's Perfect Maine® and her new "vertical marketing and distribution" strategy from dock to dish; or with Democrats, the importance of government regulation in keeping the fishing industry strong.

Thus, we advise deflecting all comments and questions if they arise about your own dreams of Arcadia, assuming you have some. They are private and crucial and can't be bandied about. Encourage your inner dreams, however, by a double dare. First, really get out there into nature. Feel the splash of salty, icy waves; touch slimy rockweed swirling in the tides and hiding all manner of creatures, even infant lobsters; gaze on azure sky; hike on woodsy mountains; breathe in air so pure that the islands in the bay seem to float on their rocky shores. Then proselytize for the perfect Maine not only by taking pictures and collecting stories but by a second level of creation—meditation, poetry, painting, prayer—for that's how you make dreams come real. Experience wonder, make salvation. You'll at last understand the power of belief. Put your love into walks and words, not Winnebagos. Imagine being a lobster: scurry with your fellow millions on the ocean floor, wander in and out of traps eating your free lunch, glare balefully at those who would imprison you, stay fresh and alive right up to the moment of your transfiguration.

Fill in the Third Blank

Sorry to say we will not offer you any choice here but "**humanely**." Indeed, lobster may be the only food you welcome alive and kicking into your home, where only warm and friendly feelings should roam. It's therefore incumbent upon you to behave to the crustaceans as you would to your children, and cause the least amount of pain and suffering as you process them. Current theory for the average home-body suggests putting them (the lobsters, of course) in the freezer for a half hour before boiling, which slows their metabolism and pain receptors down to almost nothing and also avoids that terrible banging about in the boiling water under the pot lid. (By the way, videos don't show the freezer option—it's not dramatic enough.) If you live on an estate in Falmouth Foreside or subscribe to the views of PETA, spend several thousand dollars and buy a countertop CrustaStun, the electric chair for lobsters. If you're a large-scale operator in lobster processing, cleverly combine the moral and the economic and use a machine called a hydrostatic pressure processor both to squeeze lobsters to death and to shuck them quickly and in quantity.

These, then, are the several humane methods that must be considered, for if the tables were turned, if some large, alien *Homarus americanus* arrived in our neighborhood with a taste for *Homo sapiens* al fresco, then we too would appreciate the consideration. To proceed, stick a thermometer in your principles. The throes we commit on the lobster vary greatly—frozen to insensibility in many minutes, boiled to death in a couple of minutes, hammered to death in a few seconds, electrocuted to death almost instantly— but they're still death throes. If the moral temperature rises, we may have to give up lobster (red meat, white meat, eggs, etc.) entirely. Understand that this reasoning may be hypocritical. We can hardly live without inflicting inhumanity on something. The world's moral soul does not bear close examination and we cannot substitute "painlessly" for "humanely," not even for killing lobsters. There may be no such thing as "painless." Therefore, one needs illusions to live.

Remember that lobsters eat their brothers without hesitation, that the chicken we had for dinner last night—well, we don't want to know how it died, much less how it was raised—the shoes we walk in could be Elsie the Cow, and even that the gallon of gas that takes us to Whole Foods upon our vegan conversion is a poison to water, air, and land, not to mention the greed it stimulates in Riyadh and Houston. Pity for our fellow animals is commendable, if a little unctuous. We as apex predators are much better served by learning a harder lesson: how to do everything we can to save a Maine lobster's way of life forever, however chimerical and inauthentic our part in the drama may seem.

Tourist

Sometimes a trip starts out innocently. You may not even know you've departed.

(1963) On summer vacation, a boy and his family travel to the college town on the northern coast. He's an adolescent, incarcerated for the past year by pimples and prairie, his father having moved them from suburbia to prison—a prison without walls, more accurately with the invisible walls of an ethnic enclave, and him with his driver's license still several years away. All of this has made the vast flat plain fairly terrifying. The day after they arrive in New England, his uncle takes him to his professorial office—musty, strewn with radical pamphlets on civil rights and Vietnam; then they walk the quad. Lots of walls here, of big oaks and ivy, and he could stand on their tops and all he'd see is more of the same, happily, as if freedom could be both enclosed and unlimited. The sprawling, two-hundred-year-old farmhouse his uncle owns couldn't be more different from the white bandbox supplied by the frugal Dutch-American school board employing his father. The forty acres out back feature deep woods, not sod, and canoes banked on a river, which goes down to the ocean, which he's never seen until now. Their picnic there is like nothing he's ever tasted: the salty air, the fresh baguette, the French cheese; the pungent walk at naked low tide to the island; the meringues of surf forever arriving, the slightly bitter taste of local soda. Love might be possible, it seems. Sure beats singing "Michelle, ma belle" standing at the sink in a poky little house on the prairie, washing dishes and staring out at the minister's house next door. Something takes up residence from that trip, like a new pregnancy in the family: the next year his parents buy a cabin on a river in the woods, perhaps in compensation, a refuge for the summers of his schooling. There trout fishing saves him for romance, possibly love. He is smitten by nature, if not yet girls.

৯৹

Sometimes change can take a few years.

(1998) Four women drive up for a day of shopping at the outlet stores. They do it up right, arriving in time for lunch at the fancy inn on the outskirts of town. Fortified by wine and confessions about their marriages, they vow to make this an annual affair, then walk the main street of storefronts, giggling and swaggering in clothes short and scant, taking up the whole sidewalk like a scrum of teenagers. One exceeds her self-imposed limit of $250 all too quickly, feels unsatisfied by Coach and J. Crew, yearns for something more, perhaps the anti-commercial fields and forests she saw through the windows of the inn, and persuades her friends at the end of the afternoon to take the short detour to the state park on the ocean. She dabbles her toes in the surf, has to be dragged away. In twenty years she and her husband will retire to a condo nearby.

(1975) A family from the city rents a beach house, not actually on the beach, which is too expensive for a working man's salary, but on a row two streets in. The drive up I-95 (possibly the worst highway in the world) is long, and the kids in the back of the Econoline keep up a chorus of "When are we going to get there?" which really means they want to believe in two weeks of body surfing and ice cream and the pack of friends from last year but can't quite yet, still twitching in urban anxiety. The beach house is wooden and uninsulated from boom boxes and the occasional cold wind and perversely traps August heat like an oven, but soon enough the walks on the beach, the muscle cars trolling the streets, fresh sea breezes, trashy novels on blankets, the fried dinners at the clam shack, and the intrigues of boys and girls set free of rules soothe everyone into a new, however temporary, peace, and they sleep until ten every day. The youngest boy, the one who is usually left out of the games of cowboys and Indians and spin the bottle, will return with his husband to Vacationland and open a restaurant in the upscale town just a couple of miles away.

(1994) A five-year-old girl jumps into the water from the end of the dock. The pond is shallow and the bottom a little mucky, there are weeds here and there, the ducks carry swimmer's itch and she has to be removed every half hour and toweled down to prevent it, but she doesn't mind in the least. She loves her vacations with her parents and her big sister, the incessant swimming, the treats of Kool-Aid and Doritos at cocktail hour, the evenings of reading books in the glow of the sun setting across the water, then all four of them swinging in the big hammock on the porch, to see out the gloaming. But then her parents give in to their longings. They displace the funky cottage on the pond with a real house on the coast, and the ocean is full of rockweed and potential pinching creatures, and it's hard to climb down the bank to the water, and it's too cold to swim anyway, and the girl and her sister start to retreat to movies from the video store and plead to go to a lake beach, and soon enough she doesn't want to come up north at all. She'd rather be with her friends. Until college starts, when the love of Dickinson and Hawthorne, and a boyfriend from way up north, and the desire for trees and twilit tides, and the salubrity of writing poetry in a hammock on the edge of a cove infect her thinking. How many years of graduate school and academic peregrinations will it take to bring her back to a state of grace?

❧

Sometimes it takes almost no time at all.

(1984) In a kind of unwritten, unconscious pre-nup, a couple goes on a July vacation to a northern island. She's a city girl, never been one for lovely drives in the country, more likely to be bombing around with cigarettes and Peppermint Patties, went camping only once, as a Girl Scout. He's a veteran of a few country inns, and a week-long bike trip in the mountains, and has a heavy romantic burden of a north country acutely dreamed of. It turns out to be a perfect week of hiking, eating, reading, making love. They are so depressed upon leaving that they gorge on pecan sandies and chips with bean dip on the drive home on I-95, and wallow gaseous in the Sunday paper on the bed at night, and accept Monday morning only by promising themselves to return as soon as possible. Two years later, they have moved to a house in the suburbs, married, and bought a camp on a pond where on their first weekend in possession, a frigid Columbus Day, they conceive a child in a drafty, spidery, unfinished second floor bedroom. Who's to say how big a part that first northern week—food and wine and Remy-Martin, views from a coastal mountaintop, that sexy fireplace in a nineteenth-century inn, all these and not ambition, money, success—plays in their happiness?

(2000) In June, a physician has his secretary call outfitters in hopes of attaching himself as soon as possible to a wilderness expedition. His divorce is just final, and the city is getting hot. He's lucky: he snags a canoe trip on one hundred miles of lakes and rivers. Moose and bobcats and deer and loons and sparkling rainbow trout arrive as advertised. It rains only once, on their layover day; air and water vie in freshness; the company is bearable, even to an orthopedic surgeon; and by the end of the week, he is transformed. He moves up north and joins a sports medicine group. He tolerates the female partner in the practice. He skis in the winter, fishes in the spring and summer, hunts deer in the fall, becomes acquainted with his teenage children for the first time, increases friendships from zero to three. He's been known to remark that "life is tolerably good."

◈

Occasionally, redemption beats at your door but never gains entrance.

(2007) A sales executive has been coming north for twenty years, ever since marrying and gaining his in-laws' cottage on the lake in the bargain. Over the years he's done increasingly well, and this year buys a power boat, the Sunsation Dominator, that he nicknames "No Patience." He drives it up and down the eleven-mile lake at eighty miles per hour, towing water skiers, chasing loons. One August night, during the Perseid meteor showers, he hits another boat, slicing it in half and killing the two passengers. He and his nineteen-year-old passenger, later termed "family friend," are ejected safely; the Dominator ends up on shore, one hundred feet into the woods. In the Emergency Room, he tries to bribe a nurse to substitute her blood for his own. At his trial, evidence against him includes twenty-three tickets for speeding in his car and twelve license suspensions, a blood alcohol level of 0.11 three hours after the accident, eyewitnesses who said his first response after the accident was to ask about his boat, the likelihood that he hid assets from a possible civil suit, and no remorse at all, until he cries at his conviction. When he gets out of prison he'll head far south, where they understand cigarette boats, to re-begin his wretched life.

·ஐ·

However long restlessness takes to settle, whatever garb contentment wears, it may last a lifetime, and beyond.

(2012) An executive retires, becomes a kind of landed immigrant, a tourist-in-residence. He'll never be a native, he mostly knows that, even though tramping through marsh and woods has gained him Lyme disease and an obsession with land preservation that should have been natal. His friends and family smile at, and tolerate, his split life between city and country. They know it's a bit of a disease, probably harmless, this fervent joy at being released. What kind of feverless person actually likes splitting wood?

(1985) A young couple originally from the Midwest rents a house on an island a ferry ride away. They've been to graduate school in the east, they're about to take up academic positions closer to home. They dive into their month of island life with all the fervor of parting: the clam bakes, the index-finger salute to oncoming cars, the adventures on shore with their one-year-old, the house-share with friends during their last week. They know the north, from family trips, and from the girls' camp they directed in the White Mountain foothills. They want one last taste, as if they are sure it's indeed the last. Their friends know it too, and cry when they part. Twenty-seven years later, in middle age, the man dies of brain cancer. They had revolved all the way back home, to chairmanships and professorships, and for them a Great Lake and national forests became as good as anything east, and his widow and his sons, coming to their eastern friends to avoid a first lonely Christmas, vow to finish the cabin they started to build, however unfair life seems to be, and sad. If there's any genetic justice, and sometimes there is for the best of tourists, her husband will live on in his family's labor, in the campfires his sons will build, and in the piercing call of the north.

や

Some of these tourists, these pilgrims, I know well. Others are avatars. I watch all of us drive north and think, Just point yourself to trees and waters. New England, Canada, northern Michigan, Central Park, it doesn't matter. (Whatever you do, don't go south on I-95. That way lies Disney World.) When you arrive, abandon the car immediately. Crank open your mind, stare at air. A day lost up here may multiply and lead to a week, a month, a lifetime of fevers and glows. Celebrate what's not you, light upon something you didn't expect. And if you don't find it, come back next year. Sooner or later you'll stop touring and find yourself home.

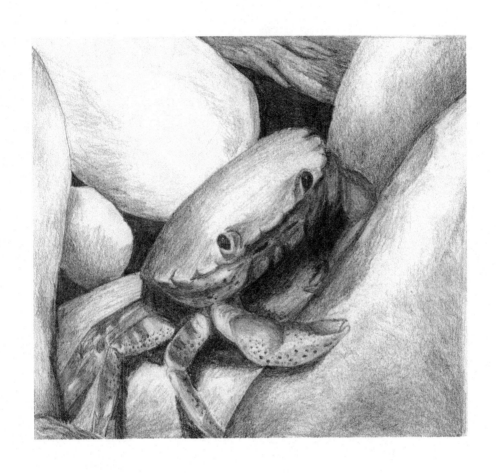

Crabs

THE TIDAL POOLS are more like tidal crevices and are difficult to get at. That is part of the adventure.

In the afternoon, when the girls are tired of books and videos and games, we set out down the shore. The sea bank in front of the house isn't a good way of reaching the water—the soil is eroding and full of small, slipping rocks—so we trespass on the path of the cottage next door. There are only fifteen or twenty feet to descend but wispy weeds and a couple of roots are the extent of the handholds. "I want to do it myself," Kate and Emma say in unison. I go first, moving very carefully with my precious train of two and making sure I'm close enough to save them. We land safely.

The shore here at Owls Head is all rocks. As we walk the several hundred yards to our ledge, I talk to Kate and Emma about the green moss on the rocks (very greasy, don't step on it), the black moss (not so bad but still be careful), the slimy rockweed (they're not going to step on it anyway, too yucky), the big tippy rocks, the stretch of small rocks that can roll your ankles, and of course the barnacles when we trespass near the low tide marks. When we walk at the high tide line we poke at parts of lobster pots, bits of rope, rubber gloves, undefined pieces of plastic. We round the corner into a small bay and walk faster on what, in a couple of million years, will be a sandy beach. I look out of the corner of my eyes at the undercut bank where the conservation land starts and the trees come right down to the high-water mark, half-expecting to see a drowned body tangled in the roots.

We reach our goal, the small outcropping of pink granite doing its best to loom. On my own walks (if it's high tide), I scramble up a small stone waterway wet with runoff from the land and reach the shelf by coming down through the forest, but now at low tide we can stand on the future beach and boost ourselves up with strategic toe- and finger-holds. The girls are extremely proud of their abilities here, bounding lithe and smooth like innocent fawns. They don't slip, although I'm forever poised to catch them.

We've timed the tide right—the crevices are accessible to people who don't want to get their sneakers wet.

The goal for this suburban family is seeing wildlife. When I walk my several miles alone, I'm always hopeful of big dreams: eagles and osprey, deer in the woods, a seal on the ledge, the family of foxes whose den is farther down the shore, the reputed fisher cat. Expectations are more modest for the children—snails, starfish, and crabs, especially starfish. And we almost always see them (twenty-seven one memorable day). They are the reward for crouching down and avoiding the barnacles and peering into the long, narrow pools, granite overhanging us, mosses and seaweed and sun brilliant all around. The snails just sit there, in boring, mottled beige; the crabs you actually have to look for, little green things that scuttle if you comb the slippery rockweed or pick up rocks; but the starfish—they are pink and reddish and occasionally move a tentacle, very slowly, and bear exotic hints of tropics and the frightening leviathans of the deep.

The girls don't want to pick them up. It's probably just squeamishness (like my own), or the tender wish to keep oxygen and life in a poor slow orange creature, but I impute to my children a wisdom beyond their years: that they don't want to disturb the beautiful little ecosystems tucked away in the granite. All of their worlds—human and animal—are becoming disturbed enough as it is. Just before going back home we sit on the ledge looking out to sea, and I hug my daughters to me, full of un-sayable dreams.

⚘

Those afternoon meanders were eight, ten years ago. The girls are now in college and it's rare that all of us are in Maine together any more. Young people want to be with friends, not fauna. Wildlife now means something quite different.

As they get more social, I get more analytical. Their absence at school has re-awakened my slumbering scholarly instincts and I seem to be compelled to festoon these meandering memories with facts and data. And in these latter days it's the crabs that interest me, not the starfish. Both malign and comical, crabs seem better suited to a world going nuts.

Two crab chronicles: On the comical side (although just the sight of a crab walking is funny enough), there's the peekytoe. Not to be left out of the famous crab parade of gourmet's delights— Dungeness, Snow, King, Stone—Maine has got into the silly game of menu one-upmanship. It used to be that the ordinary rock crab was tossed back in the course of lobstering. Toss that crab no more. It's been re-named the peekytoe (from the sharp point on its leg), not by a marketing consultant but by a seafood dealer in the down-home Maine vernacular, which was enough to catch the attention of some fancy chefs and immediately appeal to those diners who will buy anything that says "fresh" and "Maine," even stooping so far as "peekytoe."

So for a while there, it seemed that everyone on the coast was picking crabmeat in their back sheds (live rock crabs don't survive Fedex). There were that many dining-chair tourists in New York who wanted the stuff. But the government doesn't like cottage industries, and in the spirit of the times, regulations consolidated the sheds into a few hundred sanitized, well-lit shops.

On the malign side, tourists and governments aren't Maine's only invasive species. In July of 2002, Asian shore crabs were discovered just a few miles from our tidal crevices. A team of earnest young investigators from Bowdoin College found them at Crescent Beach in Owls Head. At that time, it was the farthest north the invaders had been found. (They have now reached the Schoodic Peninsula, breaching Acadia.) Both the European and the Asian varieties stowed away to America in the ballast- and bilge-water of steamers, and like so many other immigrants in the middle of the nineteenth century, found hospitality on these shores, not to mention the delicious seeds of crabs and clams and oysters. For one hundred fifty years our precious northern clams and lobsters were protected from the invaders, for Cape Cod formed a natural barrier, separating warm water from cold, danger from purity. No longer: these small, silver dollar-sized beasts are a huge hazard to our shellfish, yet another threat to an industry in Maine and of no use to the world except maybe as snacks for seagulls.

Crabs play both sides well. *Use me. Beware me.* That's why I like them. They're like memories.

ஃ

I see hints that the girls might come around again. They enjoy coming to Maine, sometimes even with their parents. We sit at the dinner table or on the deck for as much as forty-five minutes straight, conversing like adults, then dissolving in laughter at the old, silly memories of "Daddy, where's the fruit bowl" ("Right next to you, dear"), or "Mama, you have beautiful breasts—they're like mountains" (said loudly in an open-air changing room at the beach). That they then want to go upstairs to watch a movie doesn't diminish the pleasure anymore. When we had them with us all the time, we worried constantly, scuttling after them like crabs. Now we worry only sporadically—a phone call about strep the night of finals, an email saying "Mike doesn't call me anymore." We hope we gave them strong enough memories to help deal with the malign. We put down the phone and try to live calmly in the tidal pool.

I might suggest one day that we go down to the ledge again. I can't really protect them anymore, and the dangers they now face are rather worse than skinned knees. Some of them a father doesn't want to talk about at all, some he's OK with, like global warming and terrorism, but the dreams and walking the rocky shore to reach them, I bet we could talk about our dreams now.

Backward Flow

WHEN I WALK INTO THE LIVING ROOM, sit down on the couch, and look out on the bay, I get an immediate feeling of relief in the gut. It's as if viscera can be tense, have "issues." The stomach feels it first, at least mine does. God knows if other folks in the corporate battles get anxious livers, certified colons, or bile from their bosses, and how they cure them. I come to Maine. My Penobscot equals their Zantac.

Undoubtedly, the job gave me reflux, aided by the inevitable demographic that I'm white, male, and past fifty, and the inescapable Dutch heritage that dooms me to desire chocolate, butter, coffee, red meat, and wine, not to mention a post-Colonial gene for adventures in spicy Asian food. I'm predestined to gas. I should get federal aid.

Not only Dutch, but Christian Reformed Dutch Calvinist American, a deadly combination that should have been perfect for business (indeed, countless worthy burghers in the Midwest have proved it so).

CHRISTIAN: the best religion for capitalism.

REFORMED: just enough questioning to lend righteousness to your ambition.

DUTCH: Manhattan, Indonesia, the tulip craze, a love of money and trade—need I say more?

CALVINIST: since no one can get into heaven on his own, you have to act as if you could; since everyone is born with

Original Sin, you have to work hard to overcome it; you have to make your mark on earth at any cost.

AMERICAN: If America has any soul whatsoever, we locate it in the stomach. Like medieval kings, we glorify our appetites, we buy things to fill the ever-demanding hole, we suffer acid burnout. This is great for business of all kinds, especially health and medicine, and in my business, increasingly a handmaiden to the drug companies, I burned and thrived.

Until now.

In this new state of unemployment, I find myself flowing backward. One of the first things I did to comfort myself was to sort through my box of old manuscripts, which, like waves pounding on a shore, crest in critical periods of my life: the "Philosopher" columns in the Hamilton District Christian High school newspaper, the article in *The Banner*, our national church organ, all fragrant with innocent religious sentiment; the term papers from college and graduate English courses; poetry from the seventies when no one, including me, knew what they wanted to do, or more correctly, knew that what they wanted to do would not put Hondas in the garage; my journals from Peace Corps Korea, ending abruptly in estrangement; poetry from the eighties, post-divorce, about love; the unpublished novels. At such a juncture it's natural to re-examine your life, especially if you've kept such revealing (and embarrassing) archives. Is there is, or is there not, some meaning?

My wife says that Maine is my religion (note the jump from "meaning" to "religion"). If so, it's a messy, tribal, animalistic affair. There's a war of nouns in my head when I think of Maine: writing, ocean, house, family, wildlife, solitude, storms, escape. (Damn, no wonder they fired me, waving about my Myer-Briggs in glee, no doubt). This religion has no Bible, except what I write; no doctrine, except the natural laws of tide and Circadia; no church, except for my house; no ministers, no priests, no imams whatsoever (although I think I would worship a moose, actually bow down, if I ever saw one in the woods out back). And in the past, when I would go to Owls Head to decompress after a season of travel, or vacation with my family, there was temporary peace and love, just like the sixties promised. I was justified by faith in a natural high.

Now I have it all (well, almost all—just have to worry about a new job, launching the kids into college, old age, and death, the normal things). There's time to walk the shore, to figure out the metaphors of tide and waves. What does the tide tell us, cresting and ebbing so regularly? Or irregularly, neatly off our man-made time? And a wave, bursting on the rocks, then flowing backward and aiding and abetting the power of the next? There's time to write about it, too, and time to think about the idea of God, time to take my Zantac and think about the notion (thank you, bilious boss?) that you can actually cure gastro-esophageal reflux disease, however drastically.

Consider the Moose

A COUPLE OF YEARS AGO, around Thanksgiving, a moose was observed near US Route 1 in mid-coast Maine. This shouldn't have been news, for Maine practically invented the moose. But almost immediately, a gaggle of cars congregated on the road across from the swamp in which the cow was up to her withers, eating what water plants were still available so late in the year; soon enough, photographs appeared on sites and blogs. It was indeed news. Seeing a moose in this area of mild development is rare and brings out people the way the Shroud of Turin would, or Jesus on a pizza. And the pictures proved to everyone in the world (theoretically) that the human animal was also there, experiencing a moment of universal purity and worship on its way to the Lowe's just a couple of miles away. A little wildness still exists, even if it's symbolized by an awkward, shy, ugly, mangy herbivore with little personality.

At least the moose is huge.[1] Maybe it's as simple as that. Maybe the attraction is not pantheistic, or a response to untamed DNA in our cells. Maybe it's a response to those genes that make people, mostly male, still hunt mastodons,[2] even though now the hunts take place in the trenches of the office or urban garden.

---

1 Six to seven feet tall, 600 to 1,600 pounds in weight. But see Thoreau's slight exaggeration in Note 3.
2 More on this later.

It's certainly true that the attraction to the moose, whatever it is, makes people travel great distances just to see one.[3] They patrol well-known "moose alleys" at dawn and dusk. They take costly moose safaris practically guaranteed of success (such warranty is important in our fast-paced, short-attention-span tourist world, where Maine competes with the Caribbean, where nature competes with YouTube and zoos). They buy plastic antlers and engraved beer glasses. The moose is Maine's state animal and its perfect symbol: magnificent and timid, ungainly and beautiful, memorable. Even the most impatient of tourists, having seen one in the wild, may return to the city with a new take on life.

What is that vision? I can't say for sure, not really having seen a moose in Maine's wilds.[4] But I can imagine, and that's at least as important, especially when I know that wilderness still exists in which I might see one. Here is my reverie.

This half-Mainer finally overcomes his inertia and parsimony and books a guided trip on the Allagash Wilderness Waterway, on

---

3   Probably Thoreau was responsible for these romantic notions about the moose, among the many other vices he memorialized. He more or less admitted that the real reason for his three trips to Maine in a dozen years was to see them. Then he saw one killed: "But this hunting of the moose merely for the satisfaction of killing him—not even for the sake of his hide—without making any extraordinary exertion or running any risk yourself, is too much like going out by night to some wood-side pasture and shooting your neighbor's horses. These are God's own horses, poor, timid creatures that will run fast enough as soon as they smell you, though they *are* nine feet high" (*The Maine Woods*). His love for and awe of the moose—an Algonquin word—stayed with him his whole life. The words "moose" and "Indian" were on his lips when he died.

4   Not quite true. I once drove from Boston to Quebec City on a business trip and on US 201, just north of Jackman, nearly in Canada, I saw the back ends of cow and calf scrambling up the highway's embankment and into the woods. There was also a sighting in my town of Owls Head sixteen years ago, in the little pond across from the general store, but I missed it. Of course there was also the mystical sighting in our own yard, I'm ashamed to admit, and I'm ashamed because the sighting was a supposed moose print in the garden, and the sighter was our real estate agent who pointed it out with some drama as we were considering buying the property. Somewhat later, I wondered if she had a certain implement in her trunk to seal deals with flatlanders.

   That's it, in spite of several concentrated attempts: all-day driving on a number of very iffy back roads, staying in a hunting camp on Moosehead Lake, foregoing at least one cocktail hour to look for likely swamps.

which nothing mechanized or modernized is allowed.[5] His party canoes the whole waterway, ninety-two miles from Chamberlain Lake to Allagash Village. For a week there is no sign of human ambition, just the clear water of the lakes, the unpolluted air, the rivers rushing, pooling, and cleansing like sacraments, the conifers crowding down to the shore, and the wildlife: eagles and osprey, trout, deer, a bear or a bobcat if they're lucky, and at least a moose a day. Look, there's a cow and a calf at river's edge, munching on weeds. A bull stands on a small peninsula, lordly, and another swims from one side of the river to the other, not at all interested in greener grass, just swimming.

Our fantasist has left his camera behind. He does not need a reminder of what saves him, what justifies him, not even for the mind-albums of his dotage when the temptation to repent of his secular and naturalistic ways will be strongest.

Even if I never make this trip, the thought of it is enough. In my daily life in Maine the deer and osprey and fox and eagles I see from the deck and on my walks stand in for the moose; I can attest that there's still enough wilderness to sustain the fantasies of the wild life, even on the privatized coast, sometimes even in the suburbs of Boston.[6] It's a religious-like comfort to me that the moose continues in good health in the unorganized territories of far northern Maine.

That good health is not assured, not for dreamers, not for moose. History shows the perils. By 1870 the moose was nearly extirpated in New England. It made a small comeback over the next few decades as farming and forestry declined from competitors in the unspoiled bounty of the West. But soon enough "sports" from the new century (Teddy Roosevelt's Bull Moose Party, for example, or the barons of Bar Harbor) started to blaze away again, and it wasn't long before there were only a couple of thousand moose left in Maine. State government in 1935 had no choice but to ban moose hunting for forty-five years, such was the destruction. Part of the appeal of wildlife must be the need to kill it.

---

5 Even more unlikely is that he has found three friends to make up a group required by the outfitters.

6 Dividing my time between Maine and Massachusetts provides both opportunity and reason to dream.

To slake this thirst, the State of Maine instituted a lottery in 1982,[7] a system to dole out moose hunting permits. As with the lobster, Maine's other enduring symbol (and tourist draw and source of meat), getting a license is just the start of the rules and regs.

Moose hunting season is based largely on Maine's organization not only by county and town and city but by Wildlife Management District.[8] Each permit applicant chooses one week and one WMD in which he or she'd like to hunt. Hunters, both residents and non-residents, can increase their odds by buying extra chances (the prices are doubled for flatlanders). The cost of an actual license once awarded is ten times as high for non-residents.

The drawing is held each June. In 2010, 3,140 lucky or persistent or rich people got a permit. Lucky: 49,887 applications were made. Persistent: applicants got extra chances based on how many times they hadn't got a permit in the past. Rich: ten permits were auctioned off by sealed bids—around $10,000 got you one.

The lottery is skewed to Maine residents, who are allotted 90% of the permits. It's somewhat flexible and comradely: there's a system for registering one's hunting companion, only one allowed, who is felicitously called a subpermittee, and a possible last-minute substitute for the subpermittee, called alternate subpermittee. A permit holder is assigned either a bull or a cow, to be harvested in September, October, or November depending on the region, including a short season in southern Maine, aka northern Massachusetts, that substitutes for the killing by cars. Permit swapping is allowed, but only once, and only with another permit holder. Once the hunter has a permit, she must wait three years before entering the lottery again.

---

7   The numerically alert may ask happened between 1980, when the first moose season in forty-five years was allowed, and the start of the lottery in 1982. Well, seven hundred permits were issued in 1980. Moosehead Lake was already a very convenient hunting area, with some lovely and luxurious camps, and was famous for moose besides. Almost all of the hunters congregated there. You can guess the effect on the population. The 1981 season was canceled.

8   Consider the abbreviation.

Weaponry is also varied. The successful applicant may use rifle, shotgun, handgun (!),[9] muzzleloader (!!), or bow and arrow but not a crossbow unless the hunter is seventy years of age or older (?). He may not hunt on Sunday or at night. He may not drive moose with dogs, or shoot from a motor vehicle (but paraplegics and amputees may shoot from a vehicle not in motion), and certainly not from an airplane (the Federal government passed the Airborne Hunting Law in 1972, during America's last decade of environmental conscience). Decoys and electronic calling devices are banned.

Once the hunter has her permit, she[10] expects success. The 3,140 permits issued in 2010 resulted in 2,475 kills. Since the moose population in Maine is about 30,000, such a culling is considered sustainable.

This is the point at which I must regretfully part from the mind of the hunter. So far, I've understood the excitement of the lottery, "the chance of a lifetime," the detailed preparations of equipment, the days in wilderness scouting for the hunt, the need to get away from civilization, the peace and quiet of the autumn woods, the salvific power of Nature, the atavistic attraction even in someone pacific and soft like me to go out in the company of others and bring back meat. The killing part I don't understand: how to end the life of something so magnificent, so alien and yet so brotherly. Even taking a picture of a wild animal sometimes seems like snatching a soul, as natives believed, or at the very least a kind of unnecessary prop for the heaven-bound, like a rosary. I should not need a physical reminder—steak or shutter-snap—of something spiritual. I should be living in beauty every day.

---

9   A handgun on a moose hunt? Well, if you or your guide is expert at placing scents and calling moose, your beast will crash through the woods in search of love and will come within a few yards of the blind, thus easily dispatched. Moose hunting is not taxing. It may not even be a sport when the most difficult part of the hunt is to entice and kill your prey near a road so that winches on pick-ups save your back in hauling the carcass out.

10 I couldn't find any statistics on the number of women hunters in Maine, but anecdotal information from websites and blogs indicates that 95% of hunters are male. National organizations such as the NRA report that while hunting in general is declining, the number of female hunters is growing quite fast.

How the heart rends just reading about these killing techniques.[11] Although the cartridge in your gun should be large, placement of the shot is more important. Wait for a suitable angle of presentation to allow for your shot to tear up the heart or lungs if possible. Be patient, like the Penobscot Indian you're pretending to be. Your prize will come and pose for you.

Disrupt vital organs such as the lungs and you will be spared a long chase in the woods. A shot in the digestive, urinary, or sexual tracts will spoil too much meat. A head shot, of course, ruins your trophy dreams. You will have to stalk a little at least, since a moose will seldom cooperate and just drop where it's shot. However, do not jump up immediately after shooting and chase your prey; this will provoke the moose in running even farther while it's dying. In fact, you may not be able to tell you've hit it, so you must follow up every shot for a goodly distance, even if you don't see blood at first. You owe it to the moose to process its body.[12]

Having tracked and found your prey, you must check the corpse carefully to avoid the moose's sole chance for retaliation, an autonomic jerk of a leg or antlers that could hurt you badly. The state requires you to tag the moose immediately after pronouncing it dead—one doesn't know or ask why. Now pose the beast for pictures, the proof of your prowess, before the dirty work begins.

If the heart rips at the thought of all this, now is the time for the stomach to turn. Squeamish, I won't repeat the detail on evisceration and butchering and transport and registration. Suffice it to say that you'll need an impressive array of equipment, including a bone saw and a half-pound of pepper to coat the meat and deter the flies. You'll

---

11 For the following discussion of peri- and post-mortem events, I crib freely from the information booklet 2011 *Maine Moose Hunter's Guide* from the Department of Inland Fisheries and Wildlife, fifty-two pages of the regulations and practices that rule this sport, in the workman-like prose of the believing bureaucrat. A few evocative pen-and-ink drawings of *Alces alces* leaven the carnage.

12 I have no information on the number of shot moose un-recovered. It must be considerable, for the terrain is rough, and the territory sometimes roadless, and the percentage of human fecklessness at its usual heights.

find that a dispassionate knowledge of anatomy is crucial. Please note while butchering that the state needs evidence of its munificence.[13]

Repair to the nearest registration station with the following: the head, although if you dispose of the head in the woods (you're allowed to do so, along with the viscera, lower legs, rib cage, and hide, but not within sight of a road—the state worries that a tourist might see the mess), then you must extract a canine tooth from the moose's lower jaw; all edible meat; and evidence of gender[14] still attached to some part of the animal.

Ah, meat! For many hunters (who, by the way, might love the woods just as much as I do) it's the reason for the slaughter—they can expect as much as five hundred pounds of steak and roasts and ribs and "moose-burg" (moose meat is very lean—fatty beef and pork must be mixed in). Most hunters take the carcass to a meat processor, although what happens thereafter to all that meat is a mystery, at least to me; a large home freezer can hold maybe one hundred pounds. Unlike with lobster, there's no ready market. Perhaps the meat is given away or forgotten or trashed, like those huge zucchini that nobody wants.

May I say that this is also the easy way to justify the slaughter? When pressed about pain and suffering and bloodlust, hunters can always play the sustenance card. Those of a certain stripe will now immediately jump up and pursue me for this shot across their bows. Do you eat beef, sir? What is the difference, Mr. Squeamish, between a shot in the heart of a moose and a wedge in the brain of a steer?[15] And their ire may be justified. The position of a modern environmentalist, an animal lover, a naturalist, is maddeningly untenable.

---

13 Since 1980, the State of Maine has kept meticulous records on the number of permits, reported kills, place of kill, etc. It's a pretty big business.

14 If a cow is shot in the northern part of the state in November, its entire reproductive tract from vagina to ovaries must be presented at registration. The hunter's guide does not say why.

15 David Foster Wallace, in his essay "Consider the Lobster" (August 2004, *Gourmet* magazine) about the Maine Lobster Festival in Rockland, contrasts the execution of 20,000 lobsters in the World's Largest Lobster Cooker with this: "Try to imagine a Nebraska Beef Festival at which part of the festivities is watching trucks pull up and the live cattle get driven down the ramp and slaughtered right there on the World's Largest Killing Floor or something—there's no way."

Ambivalence walks the woods just as it does every part of life. Just to point out the obvious about the woods: Maine has been almost completely logged over and re-forested, twice, so true wilderness does not exist anymore. Criss-crossing today's ten million acres of undeveloped land are thousands of miles of logging roads. Access to my precious Allagash must be controlled to prevent over-use; and its depth is fed in part by dams at its beginning; and it is essentially a beauty strip in the middle of privately owned and "sustainably managed" forest.[16] And by the way, moose hunting is allowed.[17]

So I can't argue with hunters on principles—our consumer way of life has perhaps comprised them forever. I can argue on grounds of humanity—but not in its usual interpretation. Uniquely among creatures, humans inflict pain and suffering consciously, and what makes me sick is the thought of hunting for nothing but pleasure.

Science has long proved that all vertebrates, and even some invertebrates,[18] feel pain, for they have nociceptors, sensory neurons in skin and internal surfaces that respond to noxious stimuli and send pain signals to the spinal cord and brain. Those responses can be measured using modern imaging techniques, and physiologic and behavioral responses can be seen. Unfortunately, suffering, the psychological aspect of pain, can't yet be measured.

Infliction of pain in the processing of animals for food and medical research is heavily regulated in stockyards and in laboratories. Death must be immediate, or pain anesthetized. In the woods, hunters are encouraged to be sympathetic, to use their higher cortical skills, but it is purely voluntary. Until a measurement of suffering is

---

16 In the spruce budworm infestations of the 1980s, that forest was clear-cut to within 500 feet of the entire length of the river. And let me mention here that I will not be discussing in any more detail the painful irony facing a man who owns two houses and two cars and the full panoply of electronic and ergonomic conveniences and still claims environmental consciousness.

17 There may be two saving graces in all of this: first, the proceeds from the lotteries are used to send Maine kids to camp; second, if the price of preserving the 21,000 square miles of wilderness (sorry, WMDs) in which moose hunting is permitted is the deaths of 3,000 moose a year, I guess I'm for it.

18 Including the lobster. PETA occasionally demonstrates at the Maine Lobster Festival against the time-honored practice of boiling lobsters alive.

invented, no one will be able to prosecute any hunter for inflicting unnecessary pain.

But that's just one side of the pain problem. The other resides in the hunter's brain. There is strong scientific evidence for biological connections between the pathways perceiving pain and those perceiving pleasure.[19] Is it a huge stretch to imagine these pathways going haywire in the forest as well as the bedroom? Is hunting for some a kind of meat-lust, a singing in the blood still echoing from thousands of years of precarious survival, now evolved into a twisted anger at our hairlessness? The moose, ghost of the mastodon, still traverses a vast range in the northern latitudes of the world; do hunters therefore take a kind of time machine into those cold epochs where action spoke louder than nuance? In the slaying of huge, ancient, wild animals, is there the pleasure of conquering fear, the congratulation of self-survival, the piquancy of the basest of instincts?

If you believe this, perhaps you justify hunting on the most ancient of grounds, our evolved genes. After all, it's only an animal you're killing. You will have trouble, however, with explanations of what human animals do to each other in the slums of Roxbury and the living rooms of Chestnut Hill. Is this also the pleasure of pain? Or pure pleasure of death?

Maybe the day will come when the game warden, upon examining a hunter's license, will ask, "Business or pleasure?", focus the modern imaging technique on the hunter's brain, and qualify him or her on the spot. Until then, the solitary, long-lived, and harmless moose will suffer the bloodlust of its betters.

---

19   Also literary evidence: see Marquis de Sade, Sigmund Freud.

With Thoreau in Maine

Here are the steps to heaven, maybe hell.

1. Sit in JFK rocker with fir trees and Penobscot Bay in view.
2. Log on to Google Book Search.
3. Download copy of *The Maine Woods.*
4. Open Delorme *Atlas* to map 23.
5. Read "Ktaadn" and trace Thoreau's route from Bangor to Katahdin.
6. Explore your head alongside his.
7. Worry about the shortfall.

Thus I set out, Thoreau-besotted, for a recent summer month. I was alone, my only companion being the dog, the only break a weekend visit from wife and daughters cum friends who were otherwise back home in Boston working. Deliberately, for the stretch of one week, I did not use the car. I was testing an avocation after thirty years of a career.

1. *The JFK Rocker*

"I had three chairs in my house; one for solitude, two for friendship, and three for society," Thoreau says in *Walden.* One of the chairs, a Windsor fitted with rockers, rests in the Concord Museum. That was the one for solitude, I'm sure. Both brands of royalty, Kennedy and Windsor, work well in contemplation of the greater things.

My necessary condition for contemplation, it seems: it's hard to be ambitious and managerial in such a comfortable seat. Get rid of all kinds of things, Thoreau says. Back and forth I rock, pleased as I read to discover that he didn't summit Katahdin. Lack of provisions and a heavy cloud cover and oncoming night forced his party back.

He didn't push it, for clearly he didn't mind; his goal was the journey, not a rock on a cairn, a photograph on the summit, a golden parachute for the ride down, some gold medal on some grand podium in China. Nor did he make it to the top in any of the other ways that the world judges us. He joined no academy. He did not marry. He never made president, he achieved no stock options. He died young. And writers are especially touched to know that he was in debt for years from self-publishing *A Week on the Concord and Merrimack Rivers* ("I have 900 volumes in my library, 700 of which I wrote myself").

But he had work and was happy in it, and he was a success qualified only by whatever personal struggles he suffered. His ability and his need to be alone—sane, productive, tuned to wind and tree—was his driving force, eventually inspiring the modern movements of civil disobedience and environmentalism. The great nineteenth century New England intellectual loners are still arousing the armies.

Well, he's got this newly enlisted soldier. It's easy to be recruited, since I'm from Massachusetts, have worked in publishing, am writing my own essays on nature and Maine, and tend to the solitary. And now that I spend more time in Maine, having nearly retired, I feel a deep urge to retrace at least a few of his steps to Katahdin, or hike in to Chesuncook Lake, or even to dare the one hundred miles of the Allagash Waterway; to be productive in a new way; to discover what's necessary to re-direct a comfortable life.

2. *Google*

The modern idea is that technology frees a writer from pedestrian chores like library research, walking the countryside, tracking moose, talking to people. You can connect to the world any time you want.

So in my recent sojourn in Maine, I didn't have to get in the car and drive to Baxter State Park, packing up the dog and her biscuits and making a long day of it. I had Google. I didn't even need to be in Maine; I could have done my "research" anywhere with an Internet connection, joining the earnest texters at a Starbucks, for example. Who needs a frame on the bay?

Google is also excellent for pretending to write. You can postpone hard work for a good long time, skittering from site to site, laying out bold objectives to develop your angle and conquer your market. Even as I'm trying to understand heaven, the laptop wireless computer paves the road to hell—making vacillation so easy, dispatching me to the deck or the Adirondack chairs down by the stupefying water, giving immediate access to, say, goldfinches, and the shape of their flight paths. Why even try writing about the material world when the rush is there 24/7?

Yet I jam on my hard hat of best intentions and set out to channel Thoreau. Hellish stuff immediately rains down: horrible emails if I've forgotten to log off the VPN (I've kept a small consulting contract), which appears in that annoying box in the lower right-hand corner, copying me needlessly on someone's opinion on last week's crisis, and then fading like a ghost, not to mention pinging like a cardiac monitor if I also forget to mute the sound; the barely repressed desire to track the gut-wrenching gyrations of the retirement funds; the terrible allure of FreeCell and Scrabulous; and the Google abyss, the ultimate narcissistic tool, always at your fingertips.

The best way to deal with this? The road to heaven is paved with discipline. Do the same thing every day, I tell myself. Thoreau's routine is an inspiration: in the morning, work in the family pencil factory, or chop wood for Emerson, or survey a neighbor's land, or lecture in Boston; in the afternoon, walk through the fields and along the rivers of Concord; in the evening, write in the journal, work on the essays, dream of God's woods; and every so often, transport yourself to the sweep of the Merrimack and the dunes of Cape Cod and the mountains of Maine.

Thoreau had the most heavenly mix of place and vision. He did nearly all of his writing (his journals alone total two million words) in Concord, as comfortable and distractible a place as the nineteenth century, or the twenty-first for that matter, had on offer, yet he knew how to be disciplined. He didn't need any Google-like tricks to see the world. He was sustained by a vision, something that the increasingly short-sighted centuries following him find hard to countenance.

And it's essential to be there, in Concord or Owls Head, in a place you love, grounded, happy in ways you don't understand. Maybe it's enough to distract from the distractions. Maybe it's much more.

3. *The Maine Woods*

Thoreau achieved little publication success in his lifetime. The first edition of *The Maine Woods* in 1854 compiled three magazine essays—"Ktaadn," "Chesuncook," and "The Allagash and East Branch"—into a book printed by Ticknor and Fields in Boston and published mostly at his own expense. The second edition was published in 1864, shortly after his death, as a tribute from his friends. After his lifetime? He's achieved the closest possible definition of immortality outside of the impossible religious one.

Exhibit #1: The complete Journals were published in 1906 by Houghton Mifflin. They are now online. Princeton University Press is more than halfway through a new edition that preserves the quirks—abbreviations, drawings, typos—of the original. I imagine that every hundred years there will be another edition, in mediums we can't yet grasp. It is in the Journals that we start to understand. I've dipped into them and am dumbfounded by the discipline, if not by the language. For nearly every day of his life since his 20s, Thoreau records several pages of painstaking and quixotic notes and drawings of the worlds— fields, forests, rivers, mountains; birds, flowers, weeds, mammals; Concord, Cape Cod, Katahdin, Olympus—around him. From there the essays spring, ornate and passionate. And the books, just collections of his essays, perhaps his feeble attempt at fame, were ironically un-saleable. His undying genius lay in the daily discipline of the word.

Exhibit #2: One hundred fifty years later, any computer can get an exact copy of the second edition of *The Maine Woods*. Google Book Search gave it to mine, the Bodleian Library's copy stamped "Presented to the Library through the Friends of the Bodleian by E. J. M. Buxton in 1959." The type is thick and slightly smudged, old-fashioned, and if the computer could smell, there'd be a whiff of old Boston and ancient Oxford. I can open it next to my essay, quoting, paraphrasing, even plagiarizing if I wanted to. The real thing—soft scuffed leather binding, gold headband pretty well frayed, the heady smell of old paper, a real intimation of immortality—would be a better companion to sit with in the rocker, not this hard square thing consuming electricity, just as I really should be seeing Katahdin with something else besides imagination. The medium just might be the message here. But does it really matter how you get inspired?

I found as I read that inspiration is not necessarily in the text of *The Maine Woods*. It's not so spell-binding a book that you have to put it down every once in a while and hug it to your chest in selfish, goose-bumpy loneliness. For modern readers, Thoreau is a mixed blessing. Often he indulges in long stretches of the densely particular, pages and pages of arcane description of portages for example, and then jumps precipitously to long flights of the grandiose, including a great deal of obscure mythology. Half of the second essay in the book, *Chesuncook*, seems to be devoted to the moose, a magnificent animal to be sure, but not in the same league as Hercules. He is fascinated by his Indian guides, but there's that modicum of nineteenth century condescension. The language tends to be flowery, except for the occasional terse and passionate epigram.

It doesn't matter: it's the idea of Thoreau—the romantic view of Walden and Maine, the passion for observation and writing, his aphorisms, reliance on self and (occasionally) the famous friends and patrons, the commitment to art and nature and science all at once—that's so compelling. He represents the bravest attempt to make the connections between nature and spirit, a sojourn away from pettiness, the way life should be no matter where you live it. I've a long way to go to find such a place.

4. *The Maine Atlas and Gazetteer*

The vision requires a sense of place. Again I travel in the modern way but now in paper and ink, swimming in the suggestive blues and greens of *The Maine Atlas and Gazetteer*.

It is slightly less venerable (yearly editions, mine's the twenty-eighth, published in 2005) than *The Maine Woods* but just as evocative. Baby Boomers of a particular stripe get dreamy just from its covers: the front cover showing the familiar southwest-to-northeast slant of the state, following the mountains, starkly completely topologically green except where bluely penetrated by the lakes (which also slant as if escaping the urban centers), no words on the map, no roads, the borders—not just the Gulf of Maine but even and especially where New Hampshire and Quebec and New Brunswick ought to be—surrounded by the same blue as the lakes, all in all a perfect island of the harried mind; and the back cover the same shape but now in white surrounded by that blissful blue, broken into seventy grids starting at Kittery and ending in Canada, recording the gruesome tracks of civilization. Inside, there's beautiful detail of hills and lakes and contour lines, and best of all the red gazetteer icons scattered like nuggets in a stream. And you see one, the star in a circle or the egret outlined in swamp grass, and you page back to *Unique Natural Areas Including Gorges, Eskers, Caves, Estuaries, Reversing Falls, Cliffs,* or *Nature Preserves Including Foot Trails,* to read the brief description of Ripogenus Falls or Rachel Carson National Wildlife Refuge and dream a little about a world gone by, what might have been, what still is, barely.

Map 23 includes Bangor, where Thoreau started his trek to Katahdin. There's an alarming amount of orange shading here, signifying town and city lines, and you have to go north a quadrant, to map 33, to get relief. The red icons don't really start until Baxter State Park, in the glorious spread of maps 50 and 51 where there is no orange at all to be seen.

I must see the mountain. After more than twenty years of coming north, I'm embarrassed to admit I've not paid proper homage to the

Maine of the great woods. I've day-hiked in the western mountains, skied at Sugarloaf, driven twice along 201 on my way to Quebec City for business, vacationed up US 1 to Calais and New Brunswick, all timid, glancing skirmishes against the great bulk of the unorganized territories north of Bangor. Someday soon I will see Thoreau Spring in person, undeterred by weakening knees and the three miles of heavy climbing from the Park Tote Road, where the contour lines on the map are so closely printed as to be almost indistinguishable (the infamous Abol Trail, a place where Thoreau said it was "as if sometime it had rained rocks"). Going all the way up to Baxter Peak (5,267 feet, the highest point in Maine) is another mile, and no longer necessary to my happiness. That much I've realized.

It wasn't to Thoreau's either. He was giddy with the trees and the rushing rivers, the lonely lakes and the quiet, and it's become desperately important to me to believe that something remains of this, as a refuge, as a paradise, as something to pass down to my daughters. But belief needs evidence.

The *Atlas* itself is both inspiration and desperation. Its publisher, David DeLorme, sold homemade maps from the back of his van in the 1970s. His company now provides enough information, by maps and GPS, so that every foot of every rushing river in the country can be measured. We observe Earth in tame detail from the comfort of our chairs, and if we decide to go somewhere, mystery can be dispensed with. It's now easier to find oil and minerals, easier to develop land, easier to log, easier to build malls, easier to trek into wilderness knowing you can be rescued, and the very thing the *Atlas* is designed for, to find places of beauty and peace, is aiding and abetting the opposite. DeLorme was a hiker and a hunter and a fisherman; I hope he still gets out to connect with the land that made him wealthy, turning off GPS and going where he doesn't know where he is.

It's not that we must disparage the roads and the restaurants. Thoreau didn't; he was content in Concord, spending only a few months of his not-quite forty-six years outside of Massachusetts. He was a well-known cadger of stray meals and snippets of society. When he explored the Woods, he wrote with respect of the logging industry, and of fishermen and hunters, especially if they emulated native ways. He needed the wilderness but he believed that his essays and journals and immaculate example of a full life would show us how to gain the best of both worlds.

He died before he could see what full-scale industrialization brought to America. A normal life span would have landed him in the Gilded Age and what would he have made of that? Would he have dared a trip to Bar Harbor, where the robber barons built their mansions? Would the Great Woods, where the sports established wilderness camps to escape the mess they made elsewhere, have been ruined for him? Generously, he might have called it an attempt at redemption, where fresh air, clean water, and endless forests gave the illusion of contemplation, as if buying one's way into solitude kept the inner Puritan at bay. But I think not—I think he would have been scathing.

By the twentieth century, not only the rich compartmentalized their lives. Lots of people could, for Maine like everywhere else got "development": airstrips and the three-bedroom Colonials of Deer Ridge Hollow or Turkey Run Woods, Denny's and Motel 6 and Jiffy Lube, the "wood products" industry, the "leisure" industry, all of which have gobbled up much of the state's southeast and are now working on the western lakes of Richardson and Flagstaff and Chesuncook. Even great Moosehead is not immune; the twenty-first century has seen the rise of new robber barons, financial ghouls who assemble companies like Plum Creek Timber Company ("Growing Value from Exceptional Resources"), a real estate investment trust apparently not content with ownership of 929,000 acres of woods in Maine, for it plans to develop two resorts, with golf courses, 1,000 house lots, and God knows how many restaurants on Moosehead's pristine shores. The timber companies used to be good stewards, allowing recreational use on their lands, replanting assiduously; today, most of Maine's Great North Woods is owned by speculators, and the insane, relentless, destructive need to slake greed ("drive shareholder value") may well doom all of the ten million acres of unorganized territory in Maine.

It's foolish, of course, to think that nothing will or should change. To get to the woods Thoreau took steamboats, stages, bateaux, canoes. It took days. He was beset with heat, rain, black flies, mosquitoes, no-see-ums. He ate to live. He slept on the ground. Not even Thoreau would eschew the modern automobile (comfortable seat, climate control, six-speaker stereo, three hours to Owls Head), the modern house (soft furniture, big windows), the modern supermarket (we can live to eat). How many people can actually escape the new robber barons who supply our electricity, oil, organic produce, denim jeans? To speak of living off the land is almost a lie, certainly a dream. The world is connected, all right; my retirement depends on China and the Middle East propping up this country's debt. It's just not connected the way it matters, to place and spirit.

5. Mt. Katahdin

I have to believe that Mt. Katahdin still protects the woods, if only symbolically. I wish it could do more, that the great granite barrier could miraculously expand to New Brunswick in the east and Quebec in the west, walling up those ten million acres of wilderness against all but the most determined of sports. Though almost no original-growth forest is left today, it's still possible, even in these days of money slithering everywhere, to be alone north of the forty-sixth parallel, not a human within forty miles. So a miracle isn't necessary, just the will to preserve as much of that wilderness as possible and, more importantly for most of us armchair travelers, its inspiring vision.

When he traveled, Thoreau used no armchairs. In early September, 1846, in the middle of his stay at Walden Pond (which lasted with characteristic precision for two years, two months, and two days) he left Concord for a twelve-day trip. His goal was Mt. Katahdin in north-central Maine, at that time known only to a few white people, geologists, and academics (certainly no poets), where he wished to experience the "primitive forest." He recorded his exploits in the essay called "Ktaadn." The detail is exquisite, the energy stimulating. It was the wildest country.

That was the first of his trips to Maine. The second explored the vast wilderness lakes to the west, Moosehead and Chesuncook; the third returned to Chesuncook but continued north and east to the Allagash, eventually circling the mountain via the East Branch of the Penobscot River. Thoreau mentions Katahdin but briefly in his accounts of these later trips of 1853 and 1857 but it looms like a symbol throughout ("Ktaadn," the Greatest Mountain), for both the Indians who named it and the dreamer from Massachusetts who looked to it for inspiration, a totem that protected the Great North Woods from civilization.

Katahdin is now institutionalized as the end of the Appalachian Trail and the jewel of Baxter State Park, and from the pictures I've seen, is a solitary place even now. It's a wall of a mountain, big-shouldered, broadly dominating but alone. No matter that tens of thousands of people climb it every year; it still exists for all of us as Thoreau saw it, as the Indians saw it—in a wilderness of myth and magic and moose, a place to be in awe of nature.

As I read "Ktaadn" I followed Thoreau's route in the *Atlas*, writing down the place names as they progressed from English (Bangor, Old Town, Enfield) to Indian (Millinocket, Pemadumcook, Pockwockamus). At the end, back in Bangor, I wondered why that seemed important to do. A strange obeisance? Freudian transference? I doubt I'll ever experience what Thoreau did. I don't have the courage to paddle across the huge, windy lakes, portage the falls, sleep on cedar branches, blaze trails in the wilderness. I live on attenuations, pale and googly imitations of the night air and the biting breeze. I walk the dog, take tame hikes in the hills, and if I see transformative vistas, they're in my head. If I'm lucky enough to have the occasional vision, all those years of corporate training turn it into an objective, and I make a bold-looking checklist for retirement.

Maine and the Great North Woods are this agnostic's heaven: something to believe in against all rational thought, but like most religious things, the closer you look at it, the more it disappears.

6. *Alone-ness*

Recently, I accomplished my own sojourn in Maine. It was partly the sheer joy of inaugurating a new life, after thirty years of dreaming of it, partly an experiment to see the effect of being alone. There was no intention of mimicking Thoreau, no sleeping with mosquitoes or portaging through mud, and of course this was not Walden, not with broadband, comfortable furniture, and supermarket food on hand. I don't grow my vegetables, build my furniture, or net my protein, nor do I come close to matching the intellectual firepower and passion of Henry David. All treks were in my head. I did set a routine, however, and he was a wonderful guide.

Geographically, Thoreau measured his alone-ness (not loneliness, not solitude—there seems to be no good, non-pejorative word in English for what I mean) in large chunks, the mile and a half to Concord Center, the undeveloped Maine woods, the deserted beaches of Cape Cod. He made forays, then retreated, sated and revived. The psychologists would say that he didn't have much choice in being alone, with his big nose, neck beard, rough personality, sickly body. Louisa May Alcott reportedly said that his neck beard alone "will most assuredly deflect amorous advances and preserve the man's virtue in perpetuity." Hawthorne wrote in his journal that Thoreau "is as ugly as sin, long-nosed, queer-mouthed, and with uncouth and rustic, though courteous manners, corresponding very well with such an exterior." No matter the cause of his alone-ness, or how he suffered for it, he took the hard path, found his place and wrote every day to understand it. It's easy to do the opposite, in the lap of conveniences, dabbling at art, trying to understand loneliness only to lose the mystery of being alone.

Luxury could have been his. He could have taken over his father's pencil factory, and, with his inventive mind, made it a bigger success. He could have justified pencil-making as a craft alongside art. But would he have continued to write, and would his work have been as powerful? I think not—I know from experience that the comforts of the middle class are hard to overcome. He knew himself well enough to keep apart, and every once in a while jolted himself out of Concord. And when he came back home, he carried the wilderness in his head, having experienced nature at its most elemental. Is it the only way to be truly connected, to know yourself, not just your routine, to know that the atoms and molecules of beavers and lupines are not fundamentally different from your own? And to understand the spirit of a tree, un-cursed by locomotion?

7. Falling Short

The result of this thinking was a mess. I ended the sojourn in a tangle, in awe of Thoreau's life, less so of mine.

Thoreau is clear as a stream, master of alone-ness, reconciler of science and poetry. He had the talent of commitment, knowing his mind from an early age and not wavering from his writing and his observations. He was an admirer of Charles Darwin. He seems as disciplined and driven as any Nobel aspirant, except that he aspired to very little but re-discovering the old and timeless, to be a poet of the ordinary.

In my anxiety I imagine Thoreau comes back to rescue the twenty-first century. I see him on a book tour, reading an essay at Books 'n' Brews. We ask the old questions, "Where do you get your ideas, Mr. Thoreau? Do you write with pencil or pen?" He drains his pint of Sea Dog, doesn't answer. Seeing him there in my mind's eye, ugly, formidable, awkward, heavenly, I wish he would shout out, "What matters is not the choices you make in life but the passion with which you make them."

My thirty years of work have gone by with hardly a whimper. I sit in my rocker, thinking there have been accomplishments, as the weekday world sees it: a strong marriage, wonderful children, a good career, material comfort. I could be satisfied, I should be happy in a comfortable chair and a nice view. But all the while I was living for another world, for this day, and now here it is. When I read Thoreau or Baron Wormser or E. B. White, nothing else will do but to be in Maine. So here I am. Dis-passioned. Distracted. The very model of a modern major dilettante.

It's so easy to get distracted! Geographically and spiritually, diversion rules modern life. Self-discipline is a lost art. The fits and starts, the wandering around, the staring into space, the whispering out loud, the fixing of tea and cookies, just one game of Free Cell while I think—all of it completely seductive.

A passion for place helps. Writing becomes more difficult back in Massachusetts, where it's hard to be single-minded absent the tides of the ocean, and the fir trees at the water's edge, and the chance of seeing deer in the woods. When I cross the Piscataqua they all stay behind and it's too easy to slip back to old patterns.

It occurs to me that I'm just using Maine as a crutch and I continue to glance over the real affairs of the heart: what to believe, what will excite, what is satisfying. I'm still justifying the choices of the past, still agonizing over the years of the future. But the real problem is that abstraction is at the back of distraction. I can't snatch the Now out of the air. I worry about tomorrow's storm. I'm still defined by the dollar.

I worry that we no longer make connections with our animal selves; in fact, we try our damnedest to do the opposite. We're not alive in the world. We keep it out, we stay in our living rooms, watching events on television, petrified of every rumor of war, the stabbing next town over, the price of oil. We make the wrong choices of things to believe in. I agonize that choosing a career in business made me permanently distractible, undisciplined, waiting for the next interruption, or worse, wanting the next interruption. I worry that I'm no better than the robber barons, dabbling in the wilderness of the mind. Must I be jolted out of the comfortable life?

We have certainly lost the mystical mind. We study things to death—the imagery of Keats, the properties of proteins—and the goal can only be fame and fortune, because the philosophers tell us that the spaces between an author's images are empty, and the scientists tell us that distances between quarks are infinite, and what is one to do with that overwhelming information except get your own while the getting's still good?

Thoreau looked at the world around him and believed. The fir tree at the water's edge, what a magnificent subject for study! From one green needle I can radiate everywhere, into the science of photosynthesis, into the literature of *Pointed Firs*, into the aesthetics of lovely, conical essences. Following the rays as they lead you is the point, not where they end up, in heaven or in Stockholm.

But at the same time we seem to be hard-wired to desire the forty virgins, the media accolades, the rock-solid retirement. A dreadful paradox: It makes us restless and insecure. We try fundamentalism, consumerism, and war. Thoreau and the Transcendentalists dabbled in Indian lore, mythology, pantheism, but they, to their immortal credit, were always grounded in nature and self-restraint. I doubt that modern America is.

"I stand in awe of my body," Thoreau wrote in "Ktaadn." But he knew it would betray him; he had contracted tuberculosis early in life. From my own sojourn in Maine, I got the ghost of a glimpse into the mind of a man who hosted death for twenty-six years, yet who lived and wrote with such passion. Even at the end he was preparing his manuscripts for publication, and his last words apparently were "Indian" and "moose," upon which he went from the particular to the grandiose most graciously. Inspired and abashed, I'll try to do Thoreau on the slant: in Massachusetts, dream of God's woods; in Maine, do the hard work.

Deer

Now that I spend a lot of my time in Maine, and have settled into the right sort of routine, I frequently see deer in the woods behind my house. There are families—a mother with two small fawns, a mother with three yearlings—and there are does alone. Every sight is thrilling, even the flash of a tail. Generally, deer travel parallel to the shore, criss-crossing the few driveways of tar and gravel, but they also, at some peril of fast cars, cross Ash Point Drive, the main road of our peninsula, to get to the deeper woods inland, which is where their yards must be (as well as the bucks, which I never see and which is just as well—I'd have a heart attack from happiness). I can't claim to recognize any of them year to year. My encounters, and the deers' lives, are too short.

Deer like edges, where they often stop to pose, beauty and grace materialized. I see one walking on the road or ambling across it, and she stops when she sees the miniature black poodle and me, a hundred yards or so away. The doe's body is pointed into the woods, her head looks back at us, and as we get closer, maybe within thirty or forty yards, I can see her large brown eyes and those big ears, slightly twitching, that would look comical on anything else but this perfect creature. She is upwind; I can smell her musk. When we cross her invisible comfort line, a line that seems to get closer to us every year, she bounds (the perfect word to describe what she does) away.

Of the three animals in that picture, it's hard to say which is wedded more to routine. The deer seems to be following the instructions of scent and stomach and doesn't ask why. The dog starts casting mournful looks at me each day at about quarter to two; she doesn't particularly like the walk we take, so full of strange rural smells, but it's time so let's go. And the human: as I walk, I imagine the deer rising at daylight, nibbling some breakfast, checking her sites for news, working the woods, and stopping for lunch and a walk and some chores around the deeryard. Exactly my own life, except my work is words, and how terribly imperfect they are in re-creating miracles.

Deer like not only the woods, but also our lawns and gardens. The tender new buds of phlox are a particular favorite, but spring hostas get eaten down to the stalks, and the cedar trees at the end of our driveway are bare six feet up and resemble giant paint brushes on end. One evening my wife and I even had surprise guests for cocktails. A crabapple tree practically brushes the windows of our living room, and we looked up from our crackers and cheese to see two lovelies snacking on windfalls. If they would have permitted it, I could have reached out a hand through the window and stroked their supple necks. Soon they might permit it. They are bending to human destiny and will, our push into every corner of their lives.

And they into ours. This is evolution in our lifetime, I'd say, although humans aren't evolving, of course, we just "develop." It's the deer and turkeys and rabbits and foxes and bears of exurbia, and indeed suburbia, who are braving the dangers of human musk for a swipe at our ornamentals. Soon, there will be two new classes of wildlife, one in yards nibbling fresh mint, thriving, a joy to some, a pest to others, and one in forests, habitat shrinking from logging and development, fearful, skittish at the sound of our guns. And after that? I'm verging on helplessness already; I can't bear to predict.

In spite of suburban bounty, the life of a deer remains hard. An adult seldom lives longer than five or six years, and the infant mortality rate is high. Deer regularly stumble through sliding doors of houses or crash through plate glass windows of stores, rampaging in panic among the merchandise. Speeding Volvos and sportsmen not interested in meat now kill what wolves and mountain lions used to. Just in the past year, I've seen a deer's leg bones on my front lawn, courtesy of a coyote, and a mat of fur, stripped of skin and meat, lying on the side of that lane I walk every day.

No small part of beholding beauty is to deny the brutality behind it.

But then I'm faced with it: I was walking the dog one afternoon when I saw a small brown heap in the grass just a foot or so from the road. It looked organic. I moved closer. The dog showed no interest at all. It was a fawn, clearly dead. Its shape was compact, legs bent, hooves tucked in, as if its mother had nudged it into a form suitable for burial. But why was it here out in the open, on the edge of someone's lawn?

A doe often goes off to feed and leaves her newborn fawn alone for some hours. Predators miss it, as the dog did, because the fawn lies completely still, has no smell, makes no sound, and holds its feces and urine until mother returns. For a moment, I had a surge of hope. Maybe the fawn was still living, maybe the mother couldn't help giving birth in those clearly hostile circumstances of grass and tar and cars and humans, and she came back for it under cover of darkness and nudged it and licked it, and it staggered into the woods to lie low again. As if to prove hope, there was absolutely no trace of it when I walked past the next day.

Was it a miracle? I'd like to believe so. I was raised to believe so, to have hope, to fight for life. The death of a fawn is abhorrent. It couldn't have happened. There would be evidence, or a reason. Wouldn't a coyote leave a tuft of hair, a smear of blood, and wouldn't a human with a shovel leave a mark in the weeds? And if the fawn was still-born and nothing came to disturb it, yet it disappeared—it must have been resurrected. Miracles are supposed to transcend the existence of doubt. Parents and passersby, have faith, and your baby will live, learn, and adapt to the world.

Yet that poor body was only a faint blue shadow of a fawn, already melting back into earth. I know in my heart it was dead. And here I am, trying to explain this mystery in words, trying to make sense of a world in which change is speeding up and place is shrinking down, even in Maine.

And if the doe did not return, and the coyote was extremely hungry, or the neighbor fastidious, well, there are days that I'd prefer it that way, when I think rationally about death, when the only thing to do is to put life into fate's hands, when work and words don't seem sufficient to save the natural world, when it makes sense to lie down with the lion and trust in Mother Earth's billions of years. I'm not exactly accepting the cancers and wars and land grabs and all the big and little evils that humans practice on themselves. I'm ignoring them for a time, hoping the predators can't sense me. Those are the times I lie low, wordless, waiting for dawn. And when daylight comes, then I get up and stagger, one day even to bound, a little farther down the road.

Walking on Ash Point

Two Months after the Fall of the Towers

TRAILERS

The name sign on the trailer must have fallen off—I don't remember seeing it in the last couple of years. The mailbox on the opposite side of the road still says, faintly, "D. Heard," or perhaps "Hoard." We've never seen anyone there in seven years, although I seem to remember, when we first came walking, an old car parked most days on the grass. A little picture would come into my head, a grizzled man, old, in bib overalls, listening to local radio at his kitchen table, but it was quickly dismissed as soon as we turned the corner and saw the ocean below. Same for another trailer just up the road, this one with lovely flower beds that changed with the seasons, and lacy curtains, and my fleeting image was a widow in skirt and stockings and reading glasses and several grandchildren that visited on certain Sundays, again brutally disremembered, until the next time we walked.

Walking alone today, down to the water in the fog and cool air, I wonder what happened. Where did they go? Where are the sons that took care of the mowing and the medicines? Did they know each other, this man and this woman living in trailers on Ash Point Drive in Owls Head? Did they have coffee together in the mornings, talking about the loose dogs in the neighborhood, or the out-of-towners in the big shore houses at the bottom of the hill?

Ash Point runs from the airport for a mile or two, then tips steeply down to the ocean. The trailers are near the top of the hill. You can't see the ocean from there, but you can smell it. Maybe that was the appeal, that and to be able when they were younger to walk down to the shore and sit on the rocks and gaze at Ash Island directly in front, or lift their eyes to the islands of Muscle Ridge glowing in the sunset, or look to the left down the beach and the undeveloped land to see the surf and great shelves of granite and fir trees pointing to heaven, no sign of people-anything, or civilization, or the smelt factory or the notions store where they worked, the illusion of perfect wilderness among the houses of the little colony at the end of Ash Point—simple pleasures, simple trailers close to the bay they loved.

They are dead now, or lying in nursing home beds waiting for Sundays. Their yards are overgrown. The curtains hang heavy. Their children wonder, at odd moments of the evening, what to do with the ancient fishing tackle, knick-knack shelves, formica tables, stacks of *Courier Gazettes*, and gardening catalogues. There weren't any wills, let's say, and dividing up such little estates among so many siblings seems hardly worth it. I imagine the trailers are still stuffed like bank vaults with beach treasures and anniversary cards and Social Security check stubs, like my own head with obsessive schemes for when I have hours and years to call my own at last.

I will be seeing my own parents tomorrow on my way back to Boston, and they live in a trailer, and they are getting old. They have settled for a trailer park in the exurbs of Portland because it's cheap, which allows them to have a little summer camp on Lake Winnecook up north. They live for the summer and I am afraid they will tell me this is their last at the cottage. They will talk about assisted living options and their wills. I don't know how they will do without the lake and the loons, the early morning mists. I don't know how I will think about the mowing and the medicines and their precarious financial position.

So we all rest on, just out of sight of the money.

Dogs

The chorus starts almost the minute my wife and I turn onto Ash Point Drive. The German shepherd is always out, cruelly in all weather, tied to a tree and gently barking. Next door, where there used to be two mournful braying beagles, sits a mutt who sometimes adds a tenor. We walk past Fog Farm, quiet of menace the last couple of years after we complained but home in the past to a black mixed Lab who ran out to chase and growl. Almost immediately there's another shepherd, a mean one this time who barks with his fur up and his tail down from behind a Frito-Lay truck, pacing and snapping his chain in fury. Across the road, fenced in by chicken wire, are two largish Labs, generally quiet, and next to them, in an expanse of yard surrounding a wonderful rambling one-story colonial, Harold the big golden roams, now on tether because he was obviously too friendly and followed all walkers home, and with him a new younger golden companion, provided in recompense for the tether, we guess, who also hollers at our approach. An English setter belongs to the raised ranch next in line and she gives us a perfunctory woof or two before returning to her charges who are mowing the lawn or riding pink tricycles. Then we are safe. The big white house set off in the woods no longer emits that lean yellow chasing mutt (although we switch to the other side of the road just in case), and the houses with the water views down on Ash Point itself oddly enough have no dogs we've ever seen.

We've had three dogs in the past year, puppies all. Phoebe died under the spaying knife in February; we tried again with Ernie, another bichon-poodle mix, but he got into a poisonous mushroom his first week in Maine and we had to go to the vet's, parents dragging children, and acknowledge his failing systems and say goodbye on a terrible Friday in July. Neither of them particularly liked the hubbub on Ash Point so we tended to take them the other way, down to Crockett's Beach, and save this walk for ourselves.

Kids and dogs, of course, are the main topics of conversation as we walk. What will they be when they grow up? Why do they have to be so sensitive? If only we could feed them self-confidence in their food. In August in our agony we vowed never to have another dog, couldn't put the girls through that again. By October our little troubles had vanished in the flames of 9/11 and we were resolved once again, officially for the sake of the girls, to try again. No mixed breeds from part-time pet brokers this time; we went for the champion breeder, and the purebred—Mia, our black miniature poodle.

And the unsaid words? The hidden resolve only glancingly referred to? In just over five years high school will be over and our nest empty.

Mia doesn't like Ash Point either, so we take her to Crockett's where she can run on the sand and sniff at clam holes and not have to stop and tremble at the sound of every bark. We walk alone down to the magnificent view, trembling inside for children leaving home, and loose snapping mongrels, and hijacked airliners, and hold hands on the way back up the hill, hoping we'll be strong enough to love until death.

THE SILETTIS

Arlene Siletti sold us the house. We saw her husband, Charley, stand up in town meeting once and denounce the expansion of the airport. There is a tenuous connection through our Auntie Kathy, who knew Ash Point and the Silettis from Community Concerts. Is this enough to do more than look at their house as we walk by, or wave as they work in their gardens?

Their house rests on top of the hill. Perhaps it was one of the originals, built when Maine was farmed not visited, built long before the end of the war brought ranches, and the boom of the sixties brought vacationers, to Ash Point. It looks extremely comfortable, surrounded by an orchard and stone walls and some tasteful statuary on the lawns, just as the Silettis do. They dress in denim and khakis and drive an SUV and a Volvo and appear to be the archetypal couple from away, who spent years of summers coming to Ash Point and then retired here. But I don't think they are. I think and hope that somehow the Silettis are different.

The challenge in this part of the world is the idea of belonging. Even after fifteen years of coming to Maine we don't qualify. I like to think it's possible, that if we retire here and join a conservation group or tutor at Headstart, we too can be comfortable in our house on the shore. The aloofness will be gone.

Arlene and Charley clearly are different. They are old money, or they emigrated from New York in the fifties when the coast of Maine was nothing special, or they took second careers—whatever the modus, it worked. They belong. They broke down the barriers. They've found their lives.

Is there still time for us?

THE SHIP HOUSE

All of the other houses at the top of the hill are echt New England— saltboxes, Victorian farmhouses, Capes, and even the mansion invisible behind trees and the two stone pillars guarding its driveway. Farther down the hill, closer to the water, there are small ranches and other products of the middle-twentieth-century post-war expansion, and right on the ocean, of course, the bigger money resides. It's clear that the nineteenth century liked its views from on high. As does the ship house.

It's not New England at all, it's a mad cross of California and Sweden: brown, cedar-like siding, great three-story windows to catch more than enough of the view, a deck encircling the front like a wide belt from the sixties, the whole house jutting forward in a very bad imitation of the prow of a Friendship schooner. There's a large trampoline rusting in the front yard. Three-wheelers and snowmobiles used to be parked in front of a barn out back built of the same ugly brown wood.

It went up almost overnight, neighbors tell us, like a mushroom gone bad, and has been for sale twice in the seven years we've been walking on Ash Point. We don't know the current residents but can imagine the leaky windows, the floors that increasingly slant, the huge drapes drooping and sagging against the fierce sunrises over the islands of Muscle Ridge, the frustration of bad plumbing in Maine. In fifteen years, we say smugly, the whole thing will gently implode and release its dried-up contents in a puff of brown smoke.

Yet this must have been someone's dream. Someone drew up these plans, someone had a fuzzy vision of three-masters sailing up the Gut. Someone perhaps hated the white paint and turned-in lives of Olde New England. Maybe they did love it here, until the winters dragged on and Florida beckoned, or a heart attack struck on the very floor of the car dealership, or the children whined and fought and drove over flowerbeds until they won and were moved back to town. Maybe the new owners still rejoice at the bargain price. Maybe there was happiness here.

St. Ours

A mockery, I've thought, or at the very least a sentimental cliché, those little Gothic letters, reflective in headlights but not in the head, hanging just above the basket of plastic pansies on the mailbox. And the house, a raised ranch twisted and stuck into the hillside so that its side is decked out facing the ocean and half of its first floor is hidden in sod. And the enormous boat marooned for a couple of years in the graveled and circular driveway. It was clever in the eighties to play off the TV show, to dignify or endow a place with St. Something, even to hallow it in a knowing kind of way: "We've worked through the religion thing, and really at the end of the day, all that's left is the place you find yourself in." It all fit, except the magnificent view from that exposed deck that couldn't belong to such narrow thinking.

Then the house must have changed hands, or fortunes, for the boat disappeared and a new bath or Jacuzzi or gourmet kitchen was dug into the hill. Other changes were subtle: new flowers around the foundation, fresh crushed stone on the driveway. The sign remained. But something has changed.

Or I'm getting wiser.

The End of the Road

There used to be two lawn chairs set up, in the great Maine tradition of garage-sitting. We saw the old couple once or twice sitting there, eschewing the grand picture window with the big dollhouse displayed, resting instead just inside the garage and under the overhang, out of the sun and wind. The garage was attached to a large, single-story ranch, and it could have been transplanted out of suburban New Jersey for all its charm except for the crashing surf just below the lawn and the unspoiled beauty of Ash Island and the pristine conservation land just down the shore.

They have no conflict about how to spend one's last days. This is a retirement home, with lawn service and a visiting nurse and TV dinners in front of the early evening news. There are actually two houses at the end of the road, this one and the one across the street, a Victorian that says "Trails End" in a large sign over the door, but the ranch is truly trails end, a petering out, the withering of expectations, a mockery of nature.

The old couple isn't seen anymore. The house is fading, paint and trim. The elaborate, four-story Victorian dollhouse still molders in the window. They are bed-ridden, or taken away, or dead. Heaven help us if the end of us means nursing our souls inside New Jersey, out of the sun and the fierce Eastern winds.

Two Months after the Fall of Lehman Brothers

Superficially the walk is the same. No house was blown up; in fact, a new one went up on the hillside overlooking the bay, in the middle years of this decade, when the times were still good. The trailers fall deeper into their sleep. The view from the top of the hill is still breath-taking, Ash Island and the islands of Muscle Ridge are still empty and gorgeous, not colonized by refugees from stricken cities. Even the ship house has a tasteful skin of new beige paint. Ash Point is still Ours.

Yet in the wake of another disaster, this one indisputably of our own making, the signs of stress seep out. Everything looks buttoned up. There are no dogs out anywhere. I saw on the news that Arlene Siletti's house had a chimney fire, called in by its renters, no mention of Charley. The renovation of the house behind the Silettis has stopped. At the end of Ash Point, both Trails End and the New Jersey ranch are for sale, much reduced, I'm sure.

I read too much into things, I know. It's November, people are in Florida, they still have money. I still have money, and health, and time now to make sense of a life of obligations and ambition. But the nagging feeling of a future uncertain, attenuated, meaningless, remains.

On the shore, below the pile of broken concrete blocks that marks the end of the road, lies a bed of perfect skipping stones. It's nearly low tide; they will be uncovered now, and I can get some therapy. Then I see the signs newly planted, one to the right in front of the ranch, one to the left in front of Trails End, each identical:

END OF TOWN PROPERTY

PRIVATE PROPERTY, deeded to low tide

NO TRESPASSING

Picking of beach rocks **PROHIBITED**

Please be respectful

Thus we fold into ourselves, kindly asking the assassins and greed-mongers to leave us to our devalued shores.

Bald Eagles

Little Island is an aptly named bump in our cove. At high tide it's about the size of a bus: a few rocks, bushes, and clumps of grass. At low tide it elongates into a kind of ugly, green-headed squid, mantle pointing into the bay, one long straight tentacle pointing at shore (and sometimes reaching it during full moon). It's not the kind of kingly place where I expect to see a bald eagle. The shore is too close and lobster pots float all around and airplanes fly low into Knox County Regional and the occasional tourist paddles through the cove in a kayak freakishly yellow. In spite of their new-found resurgence, eagles still avoid humans as much as possible.

One August afternoon, however, there were four eagles on the island. Three came in a group, perhaps the same three I had seen high in the sky the day before, and then a fourth flew up. Almost immediately I lost track of two of them, the two adults, who must have flown away in disdain. But the juveniles, on the edge of adulthood, their heads still a little streaked with brown, stayed put. One sat on a slab of granite, the other on a piece of driftwood, doing nothing. The heirs had claimed their kingdom, and in consequence the island was barren of its usual dozen or two of crows, cormorants, and gulls. The only bird flying around was a tern, confident of its maneuverability, I guess. There was no other motion, no preening, no bird calls, no scavenging, no restlessness of either regent or subject—just the eagles' solitude and my adoration from afar. The view shook slightly through binoculars. I was entranced and thrilled almost to the point of breathlessness. At last, after some twenty minutes, the two eagles lifted off together and flew away, presumably back towards the more remote islands of Penobscot Bay.

When the phone rang a few minutes later, I'm afraid I was not very coherent in conversation with my wife in the city. I stumbled badly enough trying to describe the regal beauty of the two teenagers, but was struck nearly dumb when the adults—no mistaking their snow-white heads—came back and did a majestic flyby before also disappearing. It was if they were checking on, or keeping up with, their children. I ran outside trying to see them for as long as possible, childishly babbling into the phone. The adult at the other end of the line patiently awaited my return to this world.

For some weeks afterwards I thought the sighting was an anomaly, a holy and unrepeatable visitation. It seemed a cleft in time, a look into a past where DDT didn't malinger and poachers were restrained, where cars didn't exist and houses were modest and mostly confined to villages—not necessarily a more innocent time, just a less manufactured one. But by September I wasn't so sure. The bald eagle's remarkable comeback from near-extinction in the 1950s—down to fewer than a thousand birds in the continental US—seemed now to include this semi-developed side of Penobscot Bay. I was seeing them more frequently, mostly high soarings to be sure, but sightings all the same, and against all the odds of man-made America.

By mid-century, DDT had spread everywhere, and among other foul deeds it permeated eagles' eggs, making them so brittle as to crack under the parents' bodies. Considerably worse was the destruction of wild habitat; humans too craved dramatic shorefront aeries. But it wasn't just passive carnage. Eagles were also shot and poisoned in retaliation for the occasional calf and lamb and kid they supposedly killed.

Can you blame eagles for not living well with humans? In consequence or prudence, they build their nests at least a mile away from human activity, and the nests are wonders of natural construction: as much as nine feet across and twenty feet deep and three tons heavy and decades old. The very presence of an eagle nest means that at least some territory is still pure. The brochures say that much of the coast of Maine retains its purity, but raptors are still rare here, and what does that tell us? For one thing, that our own houses, built of plastic and steel, pressed board and cement, are almost as great a travesty as our cars.

When we do see eagles, a kind of wildness wells up in souls starved for it. For a moment, we can forget what we've done to the world. That great span of wings spans the divide. Such pricks of conscience and joy happen so seldom in civilization; bear or moose are mostly driven into the north woods. In Maine, wolves were extirpated in the 1890s, deer have become familiar with our vehicles and bold with our plantings, and smart phones interrupt meditation on the mountaintops.

When the American civilization was codified, the Founding Fathers chose the bald eagle for the national bird and symbol. I doubt they understood its contradictions. Yes, the eagle is powerful and beautiful and free and unique to America; it's also an apex predator, and will attack and eat almost anything. Yes, the FFs thought they were reincarnating the Roman Republic and the Roman eagle; did they also remember the bald eagle is an indiscriminate scavenger of dead flesh? It is fierce and wild, and so easily fallen. But in the matter of war, maybe the symbol isn't entirely absurd: the eagle on the Great Seal of the United States was designed to contain opposites. It grasps both arrows and olive branch. Can't you just hear some FF and his present-day avatar blather on that the strength of America must be great enough to fight for peace?

For this American, born in 1950 and come of age in tumultuous times, the choice of the eagle was far beyond irony. It was schizophrenia, and an insult. The exploitation of the eagle tore at the very heart of the culture, for our country seemed bent on behaving much more like Imperial than Republican Rome. What a mockery that olive branch was, what aggression our flag and seal represented. Peace did not come in our time, or few other times. What was real were the arrows of Bull Run and Pork Chop Hill, Kent State and My Lai. My generation was terribly ashamed that we were misusing our might, that just because America was powerful, it was right and could justify an imperial and wasteful way of life. There the eagle sat, on the back of the dollar bill and on Nixon's Presidential Flag, preaching war and peace, our country right and wrong. How embarrassing for the bird, to be rendered by contradiction so helpless.

We won the Vietnam War by losing it. We swore not to lose the environmental war but are losing that too. All that great environmental legislation in the 70s, and then came the 80s. Clearly, we wanted only one talon of the eagle—love and peace, man—and either willfully ignored or had no clue about its opposite: that once the fervor of the peace was past we ourselves would make war. Our own desires for security and comfort massed together and declared it. The biggest assault ever against nature—incessant consumerism—is taking place right now. The new man saves a few parks or trails where he lives, and eulogizes eagles and snail darters where he doesn't, all the while blithely contributing to the carboniferous pall that settles over the world. He's delighted to drive a hybrid car; he doesn't think about the 20,000 miles a year he drives, or the devastation in China that mining for rare earth battery metals makes.

Ominously, we've shown that conservation works. Today, some 20,000 bald eagles fly and mate and nest in the lower forty-eight, living in every state but Hawaii. You can see videos of hundreds, in Iowa for example, resting in trees during migration. Eagle cams are as common as kitty videos. And now the eagles are becoming common in mid-coast Maine too, for in October I've started to see them—the juveniles at least—almost every day. One sits for a half hour hidden in the boughs of the pointed fir on the shore. Another flies along the shore in the afternoons, pursued by the murder of crows that heretofore owned this section of the littoral. Thrilling bird: its wings beating slowly and powerfully, magnificently disdainful of mobbing crows and guilty Calvinists. It flies here simply because it can. Is this what wildness truly means?

Or is the eagle making peace with humans? I speculate that the visits the eagles made in August were reconnaissance missions, juveniles looking for new territory, parents approving despite the obvious human presence. The implication here is that conservation is working only because we've decided that certain species alone are important, forcing them to learn to live with us. Those that can't provide food or symbolism or drama, obscure beetles and worts, for example, become extinct by the thousands each year. If it's the case that only the telegenic survive, then yes, my joy feels ominous. In our eagle ecstasy we congratulate ourselves for banning DDT, but what else have we created, how many other insidious -ines and -enols and even -cillins lie in marrow and xylum, waiting to destroy generations?

Yet I desperately want to believe that the eagle remains unique. It's an inspiring bird in appearance and myth—long-lived, mating for life, ferociously independent, sacred to Native American culture—but not necessarily lovely in habit. In yet another ironic twist, in the Gulf of Maine it's forsaking its traditional and difficult diet of live fish and is feasting on easier prey, the chicks and fledglings of the shorebirds such as gulls and ducks and cormorants, and one of those cormorant species, the great cormorant found in the US only in Maine, is being feasted on to near-extinction. What's a human to do?

The fact that such a question must be asked shows our hubris, our irretrievable intrusion, and our uneasiness in according rights to the natural world. We never demand that humans learn to live with eagles. We just point with pride to their restoration, while the terrible expense of carbon and chemicals continues.

And if the eagles decide not to colonize my side of the Bay? That question too misses the point. Solipsism is the great curse of modern life. The very fact that the universe seems random does not place humans in its center. A deep suspicion of things greater than the self—God, country, nature—does not make them dismissible. I believe, having seen an eagle so close, that it's giving me a benediction. It's blessing me and my country in spite of all the suffering it's endured. It lives in freedom. The flower children ultimately had it wrong in their disdain of the state. We forgot that the streets we demonstrated on were free. We were, and still are, allowed to make our own mistakes and correct them. That flag snapping in the breeze, that eagle soaring over the bay represents both the hate of a selfish world and the healing of an unselfish one.

ॐ

This new presence of eagles in my life may be completely random and meaningless. It's perhaps just luck that I see them more frequently. After all, I can't stare at the Bay all day. I have to write and go to land trust meetings and return to the city, and my total daily watching time is better measured in minutes than hours. Over the years thousands of eagles, or right whales, or great mythical rocs could have passed by for all I know. On the darkest of those dark days what does it matter if there are four eagles or four hundred? I too am an apex predator. Maybe I should just take, and use, and exploit. The American way of life is irretrievably compromised anyway, and we're not going to give it up. My guilt is a religious left-over. Only the grave is final. Live loud.

Yet seeing that eagle. . . . Like most of my fellow humans, I'm only a part-time observer of Nature. I don't do nearly enough for the planet, relying on the science of the ecologist and the passion of EarthFirst, hiding from and hiding behind the collective actions of others. But when I take the time to breathe that pure air, or walk calmly in the woods, then the glimpse of something even so mundane as unpeeled birch bark is enough to make me soar again.

Because of the eagle, I resolve to be grateful for small gifts, patriotic and otherwise. Just a moment or two of pure joy, that's all I ask. If a spotted owl must succumb to arrows, then let's offer an olive branch to a wolf. These few eagle sightings, these humble assumptions about wildness within and without, make me see that here at least is one being that controls its power, and that it is sharing it.

White and Black

THE PRIMARY COLORS OF THE WOODS in mid-winter are white and black, the one all colors and the other no color. It's very cold today and everything is clear and sharp: thick snow on the ground, branches and stumps; oak trunks and scrub twigs dark and rough; blotched and piebald birch bark. Species and emotions are starkly delineated. Other colors are secondary, the scattered evergreens, and the blue sky if I look up, and the image of red and orange winterberries if I look back into November. I hurry my walk today, un-poetical, closed to nuance, anxious, my goal the travesty at the corner of Ash Point Drive and Crockett's Beach Road.

My wife told me what she saw there yesterday, Inauguration Day, the day a black man took the presidential oath of office, and I won't believe it until I see it myself, and maybe not even then. We had such hope at the DNC in Denver, such anxiety during the campaign, and such joy in November. Everything was going to flower on January 20. It did. We sat entranced for hours by the TV, watching history being made. Barack Obama is our president, no matter that he's half-white, Michelle Obama is our First Lady—these are clear, sharp facts. It has made the harsh winter of storms and recession tolerable. We believe history has changed courses and colors.

Yet for all this hope, most white Americans' experience of race is slight, held at a distance, like mine. I am a white man, educated, middle-class, traveled, tolerant. When I was a kid I lived in the suburbs of Grand Rapids, Michigan; there was a "ghetto" downtown that we never saw. My family had a summer cabin in Baldwin, Michigan, just a couple of miles from the famous black resort Idlewild. Not once in seven years did we even drive through. In Baldwin, in my teen-aged summers, I worked closely with a black man in a grocery store where he managed the produce and I helped. He didn't tell about trouble, I didn't ask. During college I worked in a hospital, washing windows with black men, taking care of black patients in the E.R., living in apartments in the ghetto. The industry I've worked in, publishing, is lily-white. My town has a small section traditionally black but is divided more by wealth than by race. I know hardly any African-Americans personally.

Now I spend half my time in Maine, the whitest of places. I walk in the woods and contemplate the ocean and write essays and read Maine authors: I'm an apostle for the state. But my walk today is different. I've got the dog, yes, taking her to Crockett's Beach for a romp and clam-hole digs on the low-tide sand; I'm in the place I love; the air is sea-fresh; spirits should be sky-high. But there it is. On an electrical switching box at the corner of Ash Point and Crockett's Beach, large letters have been painted, in black on white; "KKK."

Hate too is clear and sharp, arising from our deepest fears and bursting into flower. Some of us think it breeds only in masses, in excesses of poverty and shame, in jackboots and desert robes, in churches and mosques, in the bowels of group mania, but it breeds also in isolation, even in a place of such beauty. The ocean, clean and powerful, should wash it out; the woods should purify it, or at the very least make it irrelevant. Yet there it is, in plain sight, unashamed.

Coming back, I meet our neighbor and ask, shakily, almost incoherent, if she had seen the letters. She had. There's another sign painted "KKK" just down the road, she adds, and a store in some benighted town in central Maine is holding a lottery for the day on which Obama will be assassinated. "Are you shocked?" she asks.

"Yes, I guess I am," I answer but think at the same time I shouldn't be, a Boomer like me shouldn't shock easily, not after tornado alerts in the Midwest, H-bomb drills in school, the 60s, Selma and

Birmingham, the Vietnam, Iraq, and Afghanistan wars, economic melt-downs, unconscionable poverty around the globe, the constant barrage of news on radio, TV, newspaper, Internet, phone, all of it bad. And then again I *am* shocked—I refuse to believe that the place I love could also harbor the KKK.

The slightest bit of research tells me I'm wrong. Maine was infamous in the early part of the twentieth century for its bigotry. For one thing, the Klan had some 20,000 members here by the 1920s, more than most Southern states, and had the distinction of holding the Klan's first daytime march anywhere. They didn't persecute black people (there weren't enough here to bother with) but fed on hate of French Canadian Catholics, who had emigrated in large numbers from Quebec, "stealing" jobs from white Protestant males.

Then there was the shameful case of Malaga Island, formerly known as Negro Island. (As many as nine islands off the Maine coast have been named Negro, most now whitewashed to Anglo-Saxon names like Curtis, just off tourist-conscious Camden.) Blacks had lived in the Casco Bay area for most of the nineteenth century, and one of their "settlements" in the mid-part of the century was a tiny island just a hundred yards off the Phippsburg peninsula. Soon enough, in the view of the whites, Malaga became "degenerate" and an eyesore (what with colorful mixed marriages, disregard of churches and schools, and the flagrant use of alcohol and tea, never mind that except for race, it resembled any number of poor white fishing communities) and not suitable for tourism, which by the turn of the century was in full pursuit of rich New Yorkers and Bostonians. The hubbub grew. Neither nearest town, Phippsburg to the east nor Harpswell to the west, wanted to take responsibility, so the Malaga-ites became wards of the state in 1905. Some white do-gooders started a school.

In 1911, Governor Frederick Plaisted (a Democrat!) visited and took public offense (or was he up for re-election?); by 1912 all buildings were razed, the bodies in the cemetery (and a few living people as well) transported to the Maine School for the Feeble-Minded, and the island deserted and desolate. It still is, for it is owned by the Maine

Coast Heritage Trust, with a Cabot and a Rockefeller on its board, to "preserve its unique history."

So the Gilded Age came shamefully apart in Maine. All that citified money had floated just out of reach of most Mainers, and then the Frenchies and the Negroes wanted to take jobs and lobsters as well?

Is this the motivation for hatred a hundred years later? The divisions between rich and poor are just as great, if not greater. The job losses are severe. The robber barons have merely changed industries.

But Maine can also be proud of some of its accomplishments on race. John Brown Russwurm, the founder in 1827 of the country's first black newspaper, New York's *Freedom Journal*, was a Bowdoin College graduate (and the third black college graduate in the country). Bates College was founded in 1855 by abolitionists. There were some seventy stations on the Underground Railway in the state. A co-founder of Howard University was Oliver Otis Howard, Bowdoin Class of 1850. People say that the Civil War actually started in Brunswick, for Harriet Beecher Stowe wrote most of *Uncle Tom's Cabin* there. And in the War itself, Maine sent more men to fight (as a percentage of population) than any other state but Massachusetts.

I'm not proud now. It appears that our strangulated white Anglo-Saxon suspicion has always been there. The public KKK quickly died out in the 1920s, but its private avatars fester, emerging in times of stress. No wonder division into simple black and white has such appeal. We can hate at a distance; we can believe that a black president will solve all of our problems. But the space between all colors and no color is where we live. Is hate a natural condition? Is hope? Is the twenty-first century any less contradictory than the nineteenth? Do I love Maine because of its beauty, or the need for reclusive peace, or plain escape from the troubles everywhere else? Yes to all of the above and more: I love the natural world's color, so brilliantly on display in the skies and trees and flowers and waters, so simple in appearance, so complex in structure and interrelated, and so precious; and the warm and colorful humanity of the people who live in it and love it too; and I must find a way to confront, if not forgive, the black-and-white failings of those humans. For I believe that ignorance and its cousins, isolation and peer pressure, not hate, are the causes of our discontent.

There's a long way to go before this winter is over. Frozen white snow suffocates and oppresses. January offers no sign of spring save the piercing blues and reds and yellows that clothe Michelle Obama and her children. And that is enough, for now, to keep me looking up.

Rocks and Stone

I F YOU WALKED THE ENTIRE COAST OF MAINE, ironing out all the bays and coves, your pedometer would track mileage greater than from Boston to San Francisco. Throw in the circumferences of our 4,000 islands and you're nearly all the way back to New England again. And your feet would be broken, since there's almost no sand.

These great stretches of rocks are mostly anonymous, and unburdened by place names, and inspiring. Let all the tourists park their bottoms on the five miles of sand at Old Orchard, that's fine by me.

I'm most familiar with the couple of miles from Crockett's Beach to Lucia Beach on the west side of Penobscot Bay. (Note that the little beaches got named, even though they are just shingle beaches whose sand you can't even see at high tide.) I especially love the shore from Ash Point to Lucia Beach. Not being a geologist, I can only wonder at this mile of frozen time, an incredible gamut of organized size and shape and style:

> First, a long stretch of rocks brain-sized and larger, unstable ankle-twisters owned by the unseen mansion on the bluff above, where you walk carefully, using your brain only for locomotion, looking up at scenery at your peril;

> then, guarded by an immense boulder, a couple of hundred yards of gravel mixed with baseballs, sliding under your feet but not dangerous, a poor man's beach for the six modest

cottages built as close as possible, before the set-back laws, to water;

abruptly the rocks grow to cantaloupe size, a deep pile, and the houses grow as well, large and heavily taxed, banished from the edge;

a thin tongue of granite ledge next;

trailed immediately by a beautiful house and private cove whose rocks are small and washed in patterns anticipating a sand beach only a couple of million years in the future;

an expanse of classic Maine granite ledge follows, huge boulders slanting into the sea, scores of soft pinkish seats that demand a rest, looks to sea, poetics;

finally, the white sand of a pocket beach exquisitely held in arms of rock.

There's a pattern here that is far beyond me—what combination of wind and wave formed these distinct sections? Is each composed of the same kind of rock, which thus equally eroded? I don't understand this consistency, where every other shore I've seen seems a random jumble.

In other parts of this same coast, just inland, consistency leads not to stones but to stone, great rich quarries of it. This is more understandable, the molten cataclysms that formed granite, the great weight of land and water on trillions of sea creatures that formed limestone. And I understand how we made use of these treasures: Vinalhaven granite in the Washington Monument, the Brooklyn Bridge, the eight pink granite columns in the Cathedral Church of St. John the Divine, not to mention all the ordinary granite pavers for the streets of the cities of the Northeast; Rockland limestone cooked down to millions of barrels of flammable lime, which literally built Portland and Boston and New York in the mortar of their bricks and the plaster of their walls. And I understand all too well how quickly the mining ended. By the 1920s there was little left but boutique businesses, not because the resources were completely exhausted but because concrete and steel and asphalt were cheaper. Pre-formed, pre-poured, viscous—these are better business words than heavy, hard, combustible. But the ravaged land may never recover.

So these rock-bound coasts might be safe. What's to exploit? The deep harbors founded cities and towns, the little harbors have their fishing boats, maybe a clam shack, the sandy beaches sport coolers and chips and suntan lotion, the interior lakes are mansionized, huge companies manage the Great North Woods for lumber and sell house lots to flatlanders on the side. Then there are the rocks on the shore, nothing to be done with them, they merely are. Above them may be businessmen from Boston furiously vacationing, alongside them may be lobster pots and cruising yachts, but the strip between, the tidal zone, endures. There's not quite enough of any one thing to make harvesting worthwhile, and the hobgoblins of big business stay away.

Walmart on the Weskeag

SUPER-SIZING IS COMING to my neighborhood. Walmart is building a new store in Thomaston, and I don't know whether to despair or rejoice.

The crying part is easy. Not only is it obscene that the regular old Walmart—so small and dingy!—just four miles away in Rockland will close. Much worse is that Thomaston Commons, the faux New England name for one behemoth Supercenter and a couple of storelets, is rising directly on the headwaters of the tidal Weskeag River, which runs down into pure Penobscot Bay through some of the best saltwater marshes for birds in Maine. This means that Walmart will be an equal-opportunity despoiler. It is paving over freshwater wetlands in asphalt and cement, and at the same time potentially polluting saltwater wetlands through the runoff of oils and chemicals accumulating on all those new impervious (yes, that's the technical term) surfaces.

The laughing part is just as simple. The state requires significant compensation for the right to despoil 100,000 square feet of wetlands. That we laugh and cry at the same time is the conundrum.

It's the way much of conservation really happens in Maine these days.

When I first heard that the new Walmart had been approved, indignation rushed me to read about the Maine Natural Resources Conservation Program. Since 2008, companies destroying wetlands or other habitat have continued to get their permits from the Department of Environmental Protection and the US Army Corps of Engineers in the usual way, but the new program required that the companies also pay in-lieu-fees (nicely abstract wording, don't you think?) into a fund intended to preserve or restore wetlands in other parts of the state. (The fund is administered by The Nature Conservancy, thus completing a very strange trinity, especially since DEP is administered as of this writing by a lawyer who previously lobbied for chemical and oil companies.) MNRCP has already distributed millions of dollars to conservation projects around the state.

I also found the completed DEP document for the new supercenter, called *Project Data Worksheet and Department Order for Thomaston Commons*, with copies of an invoice from TNC and a check from Wal-Mart, Inc. The worksheet lists the sixteen standards that companies must address when they propose new developments, along with DEP's findings on Walmart's efforts in this particular case. Here are the standards, a few of the findings, and a touch of editorializing. (You do want to know how sausage is made, right?)

1. *Project Description*: Under the section of this standard called Public Interest, DEP says it received, evaluated, and in some cases asked for supplementary information from a number of interested persons who apparently had written letters that "expressed concerns regarding adverse impacts to the Weskeag River, construction and maintenance practices, and contaminated soils at the project site." See Standard 5 for the effect of such letters.

2. *Financial Capacity*: DEP finds that the applicant has "adequate financial capacity" for this project. The estimated cost of $22 million works out to be 0.005 percent of Wal-Mart, Inc.'s annual sales. I didn't know that DEP has a sense of humor.

3. *Technical Ability*: It's clear from this long section that the mass of regulations used to assess development is extremely beneficial to consultants. Walmart employed scores of them.

4. *Noise*: Applicant promises to reduce noise by muffling rooftop HVAC equipment and by unloading trucks at the back of the building.

The people who live within one hundred fifty feet of Thomaston Commons will appreciate the consideration.

5. *Scenic Character*: DEP finds no problem with any kind of visual despoilment. On this section of US Route 1, Walmart is the perfect companion to Applebee's, Lowe's, Shepard Toyota, Rockland Ford Lincoln Mercury, Enterprise Rent-A-Car, Shell, Hampton Inn, Flagship Cinemas, McDonald's. I'm delighted to know, however, that applicant's site drawing "depicts existing vegetation and additional landscaping to create a vegetative barrier on all sides of the proposed development as a visual screen." It's not clear what's being screened from what.

It's also noteworthy that this clause is the only place in the entire document in which an "interested person" from Finding 1 is quoted and whose concern has had an effect. He or she contends "that the proposed lighting plan for the development will significantly alter nighttime views." In response, applicant agrees to lower the height of the light poles from twenty-nine feet to twenty-five feet.

In summarizing Finding 5, DEP notes that "the proposed project will not have an unreasonable adverse effect on the scenic character of the surrounding area." There's that understated Maine humor again.

6. *Wildlife and Fisheries*: Oh, no, there's significant bird habitat in applicant's way! No problem, applicant won't build there and will graciously maintain a two-hundred-fifty-foot buffer between thrush and trash. There are no fish to worry about, fortunately.

7. *Historic Sites and Unusual Natural Areas*: Long gone . . .

8. *Buffer Strips*: See #5.

9. *Soils*: An interested person, perhaps the same one as before, worries here about contamination left by a former junkyard on the site. Reviewing, and perhaps snowed under by, a blizzard of forms filled out by agents and consultants, DEP concludes there is no contamination. Quite sternly, however, DEP instructs applicant that if

contamination is found during excavation and construction, it must report immediately to the principal's office.

10. *Stormwater Management*: We're talking water at last, and it's starting to get interesting. The proposed project "lies within the watershed of an unnamed stream that is a tributary to Marsh Brook, which drains to the Weskeag River" and then through those protected salt marshes and down to the bay. An impressive array of acronyms and forms and standards and procedures follows, whereupon DEP proclaims that applicant has made "adequate provision" to prevent pollution by stormwater runoff. In ten years let's ask the egrets in the marsh.

11. *Groundwater*: No aquifer problems are noted.

12. *Water supply*: Aqua Maine, Inc., the local water company, certifies that it can supply the 6,717 gallons of water estimated to be used by the supercenter each day. And I worry about *my* use of water.

13. *Wastewater Disposal*: The Town of Thomaston will extend its sewer line to handle 6,717 gallons of daily wastewater. Walmart upholds its frugal reputation and expects (I assume) to lose no water to evaporation, or drinking, or the needs of vegetative barriers.

14. *Solid Waste*: The Commons is expected to generate 233 cubic yards of commercial waste per month. (That's 6,291 cubic feet—three times the volume of the room in which I write.) It will be trucked to the Juniper Ridge Landfill in Old Town, Maine, seventy-five miles away, a landfill owned by the state. It isn't clear who pays.

15. *Flooding*: Floods of water are judged not to be a problem. Floods of plastic are not DEP's concern.

16. *Wetlands*: This is the crux of the matter, and one sentence says it all: "The applicant proposes to alter 101,374 square feet of emergent, forested, and scrub shrub freshwater wetland to construct a three-lot commercial development." I suppose they couldn't say "destroy."

In order to get the building permit, applicant has to meet three standards: Avoidance, Minimal Alteration, and Compensation.

Avoidance: The standard says that "no activity may be permitted if there is a practicable alternative to the project that would be less damaging to the environment." DEP then goes on to review the efforts that Walmart's consultants took—they reviewed eight alternative sites (!), not including Rockland, apparently—and ends with another perfect sentence of double-speak: "While the site that was ultimately selected does not result in the least amount of wetland alteration of all sites in consideration, it results in the least amount of wetland alteration of the sites that meet the applicant's selection criteria." Gee, guys, who's driving this truck, anyway? Sounds to me like a foregone conclusion.

Minimal Alteration: Since DEP basically pre-approved the site, it doesn't really matter that the applicant dutifully presented "a series of alternative layouts for the proposed development such as variations of building and parking orientations." How about not building at all? That truly would be minimal.

Compensation: That check from Wal-Mart, Inc. for the in-lieu-fee amounts to $402,545.78. That's $3.97 per square foot of destroyed wetland (which sounds like a Walmart price: "Attention shoppers, wetlands now on sale in aisle three"). Who says Walmart isn't environmentally conscious?

Now, all together, let's try to feel good about four hundred grand. And of course I do. I've looked at the list of projects funded by the MNRCP as a result of all the ILFs assessed state-wide over the last few years, and it's wonderful—seventeen projects and $2.4 million for 2012 alone. The program's governing principle is that "compensation is required to achieve the goal of no net loss of wetland values and functions." Damn them all. I have to agree. If the elected officials of the Town of Thomaston, and by extension its people, want their section of Route 1 to look like other visionary places generating buckets of tax revenue—Homestead, Florida, and Lynn, Massachusetts come to mind—and thereby the Georges River Land Trust, for example, gets $170,000 to help conserve the St. George River's tidal areas, how can I argue? More Walmarts, please!

Setting aside the inanity of building one Walmart so close to another—oh, and the embarrassing predation of a huge corporation on a small town's propensity for greed, and the spectacle of yet another cavernous, climate-controlled space dealing without conscience in the necessary and the unnecessary alike, not to mention the gobs of climate-changing plastic and the cheapest of sweat-shop imports on sale in that space—Thomaston Commons represents a new moral system working well. To do God's work, we must make pacts with the devil.

Trash

H<small>E'S PRETTY SURE HE DOESN'T DO IT FOR APPROVAL</small>, in
hopes that neighbors or passing cars will notice. He doesn't
do it entirely out of pique, angry at careless behavior. He
does it mostly in gratitude to the place, to keep it good looking,
to remove evidence of disrespect, to belong to it, and if a passerby
notices and nods, or feels shame and doesn't litter the next time, then
that's a bonus. Besides, a trash-picker would surely be considered an
integral part of the community.

No one else, native or flatlander, makes the effort. Seemingly without guilt they walk or drive by the same bottle in the ditch or wrapper
on the verge a thousand times and never stop. So does he, but only a
hundred times, and then he remembers, and before his walk shoves
a couple of trash bags in his pocket, not the waste-basket size—he
doesn't need that much capacity, this isn't a city after all—and not the
small fruit or bread bags he always carries for dog walking, but the
ones that grocery-store baggers rush to use unless he remembers to
ask, in the middle of unloading the cart and proffering his Shaws card
and fumbling with his coupons, for paper. The town won't help; it's
too small and poor to provide any trash service whatsoever, certainly
not any beautification program. If you're well-off and from away, you
hire private haulers and leave your garbage cans in the driveway as if
you were back home in New Jersey. If you're local or want to be, you
drive to the waste transfer station, town sticker proudly displayed. If
you're free and wanton, you open the car window and toss.

Today the bag overflows—he's neglected his duty for some weeks. Liquid refreshments were the most popular among the month's litterers. Alcohol nudged out sugar again, four to three: two bottles of Twisted Tea and two beer cans (Coors Light, Bud Light) vs. two large paper Pepsi cups (complete with lids and straws) and a Burger King cup, former contents unknown. Caffeine followed with two, a paper cup jumbled with brands—Newman's Own Green Mountain Coffee from McDonald's—and a plain white Styrofoam cup that he assumes came from a mom 'n' pop convenience store in town. A Lay's potato chip bag apparently provided additional calories and some much needed salt, entertainment came courtesy of an empty pack of Marlboros and a Hot Streak Maine State Lottery ticket (but no used condoms this month), and decorum was kept, minimally, by one paper napkin, now nearly shredded. The bag bulges; a tattered American flag came last and hangs out.

His usual walk, sans refuse and conscience, comes after the daily attempt to make sense of the world. During the walk he rehearses old words and phrases, plans a new paragraph, and looks at a piece of bright green moss on a fallen log, thinking structure and place and biology and craft. In contrast, a day of debris is good therapy for all this cerebration. Get distracted. Forget the Great Thoughts for a minute. Think about people, not nature; trysts, not truth.

Most of the trash comes from Ash Point Drive, naturally so since it gets the auto traffic essential to a well-littered road. He imagines a teenage couple necking at midnight and sipping Twisted Tea on the town landing at the end of the drive; early-morning coffee-addicted tourists from the city, the kind that demand brand names on their cups and clothes as they rush around Maine, ticking off every peninsula on the map; roofers and carpenters and contractors returning from lunch in town; the carful of guys out for nothing, driving nowhere, popping beers. It's fun to invent simplicities.

The trash on Canns Beach Road and Bay View Terrace, the two little lanes that dead-end from Ash Point down to the ocean, is less fictional. Who else but someone he knows, or at least recognizes, i.e., a neighbor, uses those roads? They're not hidden enough for necking, or long enough for touring. Why would people who live here deface what amounts to their extended driveways? And which ones would do it? The locals? Those from away?

Walking down Canns Beach and almost home, he tries to match individuals to litter, Mrs. Snow, say, to that empty pack of Marlboros, or Billy Fort to a Bud Light, but it's not helpful. In fact, it's a little dangerous. People can be intriguing in the abstract, disappointing in the flesh. He can imagine their actions but not feel their nonchalance. Litter works better as a metaphor if it stays anonymous. Insight doesn't need a face.

෨

In the city, he doesn't have to remember to keep the small plastic bags in his pocket. Every day he uses two, but they replenish automatically in an endless stream of plastic from the course of America's consumption: the daily Globe delivery, onions and potatoes and cherries come home from Shaws, a loaf of bread is finished, the last home-style frozen pie shell is baked for a quiche, and the emptied bags virtually jump into the pocket, the left one, of his jeans.

The reason for this system is dog waste, un-ignorable, malign, especially in the city. One can't imagine the owner who doesn't pick up. Besides, home owners get apoplectic about their lawns and their hedges. Obligations, conventions, protocols—dog walking in the city is a serious business, full of rules, scents, and evidence. Dogs and walkers are so common on their walks that big white he and small black she hardly rate a second look, and when they do, it's a vaguely distasteful one from an obvious pet-hater or a gush of mush from a grandmother. Just before he goes to the country and the dog stays behind with his wife, he removes the bags from his pocket, somewhat gleefully, it must be said, and adds them to the stash in the mudroom.

When the dog does accompany him to Maine, the protocol changes. They still walk twice a day, of course, as demanded by their need for a schedule, but he carries bags only for an emergency. He attempts to follow a greener way of life up here, and she would agree

Trash ෨ 137

if she could. They walk the lanes and the road, and sometimes she remembers to be green and add her fertilizer near the woods through which the lanes wend, but sometimes she forgets and uses, or tries to use, the lawns or bushes of the few houses they pass. He trusts he's such a regular sight after fifteen years of walking that a little waste on a lawn would be tolerated. But still . . . city mores persist. He doesn't want to be seen as a nuisance. He wants to keep every advantage when he's in the country.

But of course he's a sight, he knows that he must be the subject of speculation: a very tall man, dressed in clothes from away, walking a black miniature poodle. This is not a Maine kind of dog, not a Lab or a setter or a Ridgeback. She doesn't have the poofy poodle cut, but still. One memorable morning, before the town leash laws were widely enforced, he remonstrated with the owner of a German shepherd, off-leash and menacing, and was called a "fucking faggot" for his troubles. He knows the man was hardly representative of the town, especially as he appeared to be drunk at ten o'clock in the morning. But just to be sure of safety, he has made it a point ever since to wave at each car and pickup that passes him on the roads (in a restrained, manly way, of course, a sort of index-finger waggle at the end of a slightly raised arm), a friendly gesture that someone might remember, that might prove useful to him in a time of need.

⚬

He wouldn't think about picking up debris in the city. He lives in a well-ordered suburb, of course, where there isn't much loose of anything blowing around, not even morals, but occasionally a can or a cup or junk mail gets tossed, or falls when the garbage truck with the big grasping arm slightly fumbles. To maintain a civilization when everyone's on top of each other requires personal space, or property space; any trespass of which, including a simple act of trash kindness, seems a violation of the covenant of non-involvement. Better to walk on by.

His neighbor polices the big park nearby, half of which is devoted to nature as woods, half of which is devoted to humans as sports fields; that's correct behavior, that's pretending the city is redeemable, is something lovely. But on private property—a man in America must be free to pick up and put down what he wishes, without assistance.

This is also why walkers in the city generally don't wave, or speak a greeting, or meet one's eye, or even move over on the sidewalk. They carry their inviolability with them. A personal wasteland is not to be breached.

જ

By noon he's back at the house and puts the Ash Point trash in the big blue garbage barrel, except of course for the four recyclables. The joys of walking in nature, without that rule-making dog, no trash left in sight, have brimmed over—innocent trees, sky merging with island and bay, the lichen and moss of the ages, the lives of deer and grouse and pileated woodpecker moving in the woods and sometimes intersecting with his. They inspire him to madness. That is, he thinks he doesn't need anything else.

But he does, and those joys should be his real salvation, those walks should put him in the way of possible community. Unfortunately, in this part of Maine—a rather ordinary part, no big tourist attractions—very few people walk. They'll drive to the lighthouse or the landing at Ash Point to look at the ocean; they'll drive to the neighboring city for groceries and beer, movies and fast food; but almost no one walks except a few older women in the middle of the day who are intent on exercise and care only to nod pleasantly; a stocky man with a crooked walk who is seen everywhere, at all times of day, as if he's working off his handicap, and who gruffly says hello; and neighbors walking *their* dogs: all these walkers are fine and good but afford little chance of empathy.

Some days he does hope for more. Perhaps the inhabitants of that low, rambling yellow house sprawling so comfortably on the hill will emerge and engage. Perhaps when the Old Homestead is open, Wednesday afternoons in the summer, 2:00 to 4:00, he'll interrupt his walk and ask the ladies of the Historical Society a question or two about town characters. Later, he tells himself, next week.

On the computer, he captures a phrase or two for tomorrow's session, checks email from the city, then moves from the rocker to the deck, with book and lunch, to the fresh cool air that the most recent storm has brought. He tries to think about the contrasts of his two lives: country vs. city, clean vs. dirty, quiet vs. loud, plants and animals vs. concrete and tar, locals vs. people from away. But often it all seems like escape, or a placid vacillation between two points and in the swinging back and forth he lands nowhere.

That storm banged through and cleaned out humid thoughts and blew down trees and, from the cemetery on Ash Point Drive, tore an American flag off a grave. Tattered and ripped, the flag ended up in his trash bag. Standing at the garbage barrel, he wasn't quite sure for a moment what to do with it, this symbol of success, this unabashed and heartfelt way to honor the dead, this rallying point for rural lives. At one time, in the sixties, he would have calmly trashed it but now he's not so sure. America promised him liberty but gave him choice.

Several flags remain in the cemetery, some freshly planted, some hanging on by a thread. He'll watch for them every day, analyze their progress to waste, pick them up when they tear free, perhaps fold them gently before putting them in the bag for the dump. He'll think more about the promises of the country, and the Country. He'll resolve to understand the people of this town—how to live in the moment, how to live more easily with the dead. He'll walk every road and lane of his adopted community, loitering near yards, putting himself in the way, eulogizing a losing way of life, hoping to be more responsible for his mortality.

Average Fuel

THE STRUGGLE WITH MY CAR'S ECON has been going on for a year now, with one more to go on the leash, I mean lease. ECON's been good to me, performing above expectations. Whether it's been good *for* me is another question, judging by the amount of attention it demands and the somewhat tawdry nature of the relationship.

It's hard to ignore, that big green button called ECON on the far left side of the dash. When I pushed it the first time, nothing appeared to happen except an announcement, in the "multi-information display," that ECON was on. Nothing changed, not on the dashboard nor yet in behavior or conscience. I was forced to the owner's manual for enlightenment: the ECON button, it said, makes the accelerator pedal less responsive and partially thwarts the A/C, among other, more arcane mechanical depressions. In other words, it's a simple yes/no decision. I save some fossil fuel, or I don't—morality at the push of a button.

If only Honda had left it at that. But no, they had to go and make good and evil obvious. They had to make me feel guilty every minute of drive time. I can no longer blithely burn up the earth as I drive to and from my virtuous second life in Maine.

In short, I cannot not look at the dashboard.

I should first set the stage and say that the dash is almost entirely digital. I can get to a clock face that looks analog, but it requires several punches at the Menu. All the rest of the indicators are numbers and graphics, mostly white but with shadings of blue here and there. Very hip, very appealing, including no fewer than three gauges to indicate fuel consumption.

The first one sits squarely in front of the driver, and since it's designed for a younger, visual generation, I've learned to ignore it. Two coaching bars (so-called in the owner's manual) straddle the digital speedometer like traffic lanes, aiming at some vanishing point of perspective and symbolizing, I presume, the lure of the open road. Upon acceleration the bars turn a violent blue like nothing in nature; thence they retreat to an aquamarine state of Caribbean grace as performance improves; and they finish on the bright green of trees in spring (way too obvious, Honda) when performance is exemplary, say coasting downhill. A pretty picture indeed, like two lava lamps firing and fading, but not a serious tool for guilty Boomers.

The other two indicators grab attention as if the dash featured a peep show. The one just to the right of the coaching bars is a horizontal line of lozenges running on a scale marked zero, thirty-five, and seventy miles per gallon, each lozenge slightly tilted to the left. The line lights up and advances right when I'm being a good boy, and blinks out to the left when I'm transgressing. This happens more or less in real time, an instant judgment on my abilities, my world and life view, and probably my Calvinistic upbringing. The lozenges queasily fall to nearly zero as ECON tries to climb a hill, they triumphantly butt up against seventy as we coast to a stop for a red light. After a year of staring at them, I see lozenges in my sleep. They bear down on me like eighteen-wheelers.

The third and final indicator is the most terrible. Whereas Indicator #2 is imprecise, with but three stages of godliness, Indicator #3 destroys any vestige of happy ignorance. A real digital read-out refreshes itself several times a minute, a precise and brutal miles per gallon that celebrates or chastises down to the tenth. It shows virtue calculated over distance: real Average Fuel, the fleeting tyranny of the accelerator extended through time. That's the number I'm fixed on. At the start of every trip, and sometimes in the middle just to test the variables, I re-set Indicator #3 (Trip A or B!) to measure how my performance is evolving. Possibly, ECON is altering my genes as I drive.

My worst performance, besides the zero of a traffic jam or stop light, has been 5.3 mpg as we groan uphill, my best a Hallelujah of 199.9 mpg while coasting down on a re-set. ECON records no higher rate, to protect vocal cords perhaps.

ECON achieves some of its miracles by having no power. As I approach that hill in Waldoboro, I no longer use the passing lane but immediately slide to the right. Everyone overtakes me. Maybe they laugh at the old guy in his little car. To their minds' eyes I might as well add hunching forward and gripping the steering wheel with hands at ten and two. I've already got the graying hair.

I should also say that while I may be slightly obsessed with ECON, I've not yet succumbed to the full menu of hypermiling. Yes, I observe the speed limit, eschew the A/C, anticipate stops miles in advance, and generally acknowledge that the brake is the enemy. But I'm not yet so ardent as to woo ECON into any more of the 109 tips I found on one website. For example, I won't be attempting #55, Engine Off Coasting (EOC), which advises: "In non-hybrids, EOC is considered an advanced technique and should not be attempted until the skill developed (sic) away from traffic. In addition, coasting with the engine off is illegal in some areas." On the other hand, maybe I will try #58, Pulse and Glide, or even #108, Listen to Slower Music, when I'm feeling bad about exceeding fifty-five on the turnpike and using cruise control on hills.

Other drivers of my ECON, of course, set the enterprise back. One heavy-footed daughter reduced ECON to tears (and 35 mpg) following a trip from Boston to Deer Isle. Dear, un-hypermiling spouse drives around town and I see an alarming decline in Average Fuel, although in her defense, ECON suffers greatly in stop-and-start driving even under more fanatic ministrations. And therefore, yes, I spend the whole four hours driving to or from Maine regaining respectability, obsessing over tenths, despairing as Waldoboro drops me a whole point, cheering as I coast down to the toll booth in Kittery and get back 0.4. And I've not figured out why I seem to get better mileage coming back south to Massachusetts. It can't be. It's the same route, same hills and traffic lights. I must not be accounting properly for winter blends of gas, under-inflation of tires in the cold, head- or tailwinds, the number of books I've packed, the number of Trader Joe's frozen entrees in the ice chest, or how anxious I am to compensate for that day's news about climate change.

So this is personal. I look at those damn gauges several times a minute. Somehow Honda has persuaded me that Earth's fate is in my hands.

And I am doing far better than most people. Those ads that tout twenty-four mpg for the latest cross-over? I scoff. I'm pushing forty-five, Bub. At these rates I don't have to drive an over-priced hybrid, with its battery like a time bomb, dirty to make, impossible to recycle. And I've plenty of techniques in reserve if guilt gets worse.

Not only that, but *my* 12,000 miles a year are justified, for I'm escaping to Maine twice a month to volunteer for a land trust, and that means saving land and sequestering carbon if nothing else. And if everyone were as conscientious, committed, and careful as I (so goes the liberal plaint), wow, we could save the planet.

Ridiculous, of course. What one person does means almost nothing. It's already too late. These words I write could lighten a thousand lead feet and make a difference but vanishingly small. ECON is an atom in a slowly exploding mushroom cloud. That traffic jam on Route 128, going nowhere but still burning, is repeated a thousand times a day across the world. Think about a cruise ship: the average trip from Boston to Bermuda consumes a quarter million gallons of fuel, advancing thirty feet for each gallon burned.

Am I not much better than all that? Yet I obsess. Western life is a long series of compromises and conundrums: boycotting Walmart means fabric workers in Bangladesh lose their jobs; a brand-new efficient house may never save enough energy to overcome the amount needed to build it in the first place; nearly every bite of our food reeks of the carbon exhaust of combines, semis, and jets; every soft comfort has a hard cost; just driving a car is an abomination. I can't (or won't) do the right thing and live hermit-like in Maine. Why bother?

Yet I obsess. I note ECON's every tenth of change, seeing visions of that trip on the flat, hot highways of the Midwest last year when we nearly topped the magic mountain of fifty mpg. But in the hilly East we fail. Our consumption gallops.

No wonder I worry. The news is full of the wonders of natural gas, so incredibly abundant as shale gas under the land and methane ice under the coasts that it may be a larger resource than all other carbon fuels combined. Fantastic? No—we'll burn it all.

So I obsess on ECON. Only two icons show on the systems part of the dashboard, and one of those winks out when the engine warms up. Until disaster actually happens, all those other indicators of doom—brake warnings and shift malfunctions and systems failure and engine overheating—stay invisible, deferring to the one constant green, creepy half-tree, half-human thing that's lit when ECON is on. Let's just drive along as the planet gets sick and overheats, just be green and everything will be OK.

And yet I scan ECON's gauges, every few seconds. Of course, I could turn Average Fuel off. But I won't. I need to know I'm trying as best I can. I need to be forced to know I'm making a difference, however minuscule. I need to know that whatever I do is almost completely inconsequential to the world, yet still matters in some way. I need to be better than average, at least in a car, spending our planet's inheritance.

I'm not released until the car is turned off (Tip #72, Turn key off, then shift to Park). Whew. I can relax again. Other demons of consumption don't pester quite so insistently.

Lupine

ESPITE SOME TWENTY YEARS OF ESCAPING to Maine as often as is seemly, my wife and I can count on the fingers of one hand the number of times we've actually seen fields of lupine (except cruelly in the depths of winter, in the eye-tease that is *Down East Magazine*): wild, glorious lupine, in every shade of red, white, pink, purple, blue. There was even a prime example of its exuberance at the top of our road, a quarter acre at least, but in all those Mays and Junes of our daughters' play dates, piano recitals, school sports, community service, college visits, proms, final exams, and those dag-blasted Memorial Day soccer tournaments as far away from Boston as Cape Cod we saw the field in full glory once, maybe twice, and then three years ago the landowner mowed it all down for the sake of something to do, I expect, with his new riding Kubota.

Or was it because he had the lupines tested and they turned out to be one of the poisonous species? Anything is possible with this strange and wonderful plant.

Lupine is one of the things that symbolizes Maine for me, and in preparation for the joy of seeing more of it upon sending the kids off to college and getting ready to retire, I recently did some reading about it. All I knew about the flower before I started was its spring-time profligacy and the stubbornness for the rest of the year of the one example we have down in our ocean-side garden, well, not exactly stubbornness, but more of a sly and fecund ability to pop new stalks a foot or two away from Mother Plant. Clearly,

Mother's sole purpose in life is to stalk the asphodel and smother it. The beach rose right next to the garden has the same murderous intent—it's tempting to let both rose and lupine shoot out their tap roots and see who wins.

I'd bet on the lupine, long-term certainly: it boasts hundreds of species, hybrids and cultivars; it thrives in poor soil (it's a legume, surprisingly, and legumes fix nitrogen, making their own fertilizer); it propagates easily but transplants with difficulty; yes, some species are full of alkaloids, but others, like the white lupin of Europe and the Middle East, produce delicious, oily seeds "with the full range of essential amino acids" (source long lost). For years agronomists have wanted to dispense with the temperamental soybean, which requires too much water and fertilizer, and warm weather to boot. Lupine would be a wonderful substitute, they say, and I imagine millions of acres of wondrous, frost-tolerant, red-white-and-blue flowers blanketing the middle of the country from Dakota to Texas. To encourage conversion, the Department of Agriculture should mandate a patriotic name. Like Flag Bean. The farmers could plant it in stripes.

Alarmingly, I also discover that the Maine lupine and the Texas bluebonnet are closely related. This dire thought makes me think of that great, unexplained mystery of life up here. Why do the George Herbert Walker Bushes come to Maine?

I could argue that Walker's Point and Kennebunkport (traffic jams, cigarette boats, barricades and gates, Secret Service) are more like Texas than Maine. I could argue that GHWB goes because he inherited the place from his parents Prescott Bush and Dorothy Walker (who got it from Daddy George Walker, the St. Louis banker who built it), that son W dutifully attends only because his daddy might yet change his will and leave it all to Jeb. The view and the house are magnificent, this alone would impress the oiled and jaded. But the Bushes clearly like the place, even W, what with the recent visits of the Putins and the Sarkozys, and there must be something in the character of a Bush that longs to forsake the dry ranches and back-slappers of Houston, if only for a few days a year. Still, I really don't see how a Massachusetts liberal like me and a Texas conservative like Bush can share the same pleasure. Or does Maine have the power to redeem even the most stubborn and shallow of souls?

People once thought that *Lupinus* must have a voracious appetite for nutrients, considering what poor soil it grows in. Hence the wolf-like name. But the opposite is true; it enriches the soil. Perhaps George W has a similar problem. Under that goofy skin lies a serious soul—in that strange family (the teeny-bopper twins, faded Jeb, shady Neil, anodyne Marvin and Dorothy, disgraced Barbara, and a father whose reputation gains only in contrast to his son's) there is love and compassion—the war-monger finds peace in coastal Maine.

Nah—you have to bring something to heaven to get in.

The explanation for his presence in Maine may be scientific, some kind of brute genetic divergence, like lupine and bluebonnet, or Dick and Sally Cheney. These Republicans do seem to propagate with difficulty, transplant with ease.

But I think it's a little more complicated, that deep down he imagines himself a modern Thoreau (OK, minus the toadyism, the politics, the thirst for oil, the fractured English). He's adventurous, has a sneaking respect for self-reliance, and is never happier than when clearing a little sagebrush around his own Walden. If W were to read books, he would nod approvingly at this passage from Thoreau's Journal, June 5, 1852, for it could apply to Texas as well as Maine: "The lupine is now in its glory . . . the earth is blued with them . . . You passed along here, perchance, a fortnight ago, and the hillside was comparatively barren. But now you come and these glorious redeemers appear to have flashed out here all at once. Who planted the seeds of lupines in the barren soil? Who watereth the lupines in the fields?"

In his wintry dotage, contemplating the Almighty, George might have a brief moment of regret for the performances of his spring and summer. But he won't retire to Maine to heal his soul, he can't go truly native, he won't be redeemed of his sins by faith and family and give something back. He'll go to Crawford to punch oil men on the arm and shoot tame grouse with politicians. His world will not have changed, not even because of a couple of weeks a year at Walker's Point. "We are in great haste," Thoreau said, "to construct a magnetic telegraph from Maine to Texas; but Maine and Texas, it may be, have nothing important to communicate." At last, something on which W and I, both about to retire, at our opposite ends of the *Lupinus* wire, will agree.

Revelations in the Maine Woods

SOMETIMES THESE FEEL like the last days. No wonder we want to channel Thoreau and escape to the Wildness, pulling cedar boughs around us for comfort at night, or sitting lonely and safe on a ledge above a lake. Jihad has no meaning in the woods. Black water deepens, in cool profundity, and allows no such thing as a mercenary. The currency there is carbon, not ambition. Greed for fresh air sucks it deep into the lungs, snorts the smell of humus and moss of the forest floor.

Last days are nothing new under the sun. Utopias spring up, winter down. Heretics and hermits proclaim and damn. All will be revealed upon the breaking of the seventh seal.

Except that we don't believe in revelations. Belief is just a national park of the mind.

Except that hope survives the absence of belief, even today, especially today, and I myself will believe in hope until hope is gone.

※

A particularly peculiar fact about Maine is that one-third of the state is unorganized, a swath of ten million acres (forests and lakes and mountains in the west, plains and farms in the east) that has no local governance, whose development is administered by the seven men and women of the Land Use Regulation Commission in Augusta. Of these territories, the deep North Woods covers some three million acres, and in 1994 a group in Maine, alarmed by developments, began promoting the idea of a national park to preserve it. Those North Woods is an immense area—if it were squared into a block, each side would measure nearly seventy miles—the largest undeveloped forest east of the Rockies. The model is nearby Baxter State Park, 200,000 acres of wilderness surrounding Mt. Katahdin and protected forever.

It's a sign of our times that I'd call five thousand square miles immense. Native people wouldn't have. Roaming without fences or LURCs, they lived in harmony there for thousands of years. White people are different; we threaten the survival of the woods after only a few hundred.

We started clearing the land almost immediately upon arrival. Pilgrims and traders and fishermen carved villages out of the coast. Farmers moved inland, gunning for Indians. In the eighteenth century British surveyors roamed the colonies, chopping King George's mark of the broad arrow into stately white pines, commandeering them for the masts of his ships. By the nineteenth century most of New England's forests were gone, either to timber or pasture. Big timber companies formed out of the little ones, and they have cut and slashed at the forest's innards for two centuries now. In the Gilded Age and beyond, wealthy "sports" from the big cities rusticated in camps and cottages. The prosperity spawned by winning two world wars in the twentieth century also spawned the invasion of middle-class Americans on vacation. And now in the twenty-first century, now it will get worse.

For while the timber companies used to own most of Maine, at least they were relatively benign, allowing hunting and fishing and hiking on their land and often thinking about sustainability (90% of the state has come back to forest). Then, inevitably, business found cheap trees and cheaper labor in Asia, Africa, and South America. The investment value of Maine's trees went down, and the money men, sensing bargains, came calling.

Upon which the land became more than just trees. It was transformed into real estate, and a web of Real Estate Investment Trusts and international finance now owns most of the Maine woods. What will they do with their assets? How will they exploit what's left of the wilderness?

It seems clear to me. Let a thousand Plum Creeks bloom.

The Plum Creek Timber Company, American's largest private land owner, bought up nearly a million acres near and around Moosehead Lake over the past few years. (Moosehead is the large wilderness lake that Thoreau, when he viewed it from the top of Mt. Kineo, compared to "a gleaming silver platter at the end of the table.") Plum Creek wants to make that metaphor tangible, lots of platters on lots of tables, proposing nearly a thousand house lots and a couple of golf courses and hotels and several restaurants, no doubt themed or franchised, for the lakeshore. Moosehead has four hundred miles of shoreline, almost of all of it shining-pure and undeveloped. It's a treasure, but what kind, and for whom?

Disclosure: Even in Thoreau's time, Moosehead was being developed. He didn't hike there; from Concord, he took a train to Bangor and a stagecoach to Greenville. And he toured the lake by noisy, dirty steamboat, like any tourist.

Fuller disclosure: I too am a property owner in Maine. I owned a camp on a lake, and now a house on the ocean. So why should I object if 975 future mortgagers build their own Zions on Moosehead?

Furthermore, the North Woods is hardly wilderness anymore, having been exploited for centuries. There are 31,000 miles of logging roads that muddy the hooves of moose and deer. People use the woods, hunting and fishing and skiing and hiking and snowmobiling and swimming and communicating with gods. They scratch a living from felled wood, or from tourists, and soon from wind power. It's a hard life. The young don't stay around—there's little work, nothing to do.

Yet Moosehead seems a crossroads. LURC worked hard (the Plum Creek proposals stretched over five years and multiple incarnations, the most recent a thousand pages). The conservation groups worked hard. Plum Creek worked hard and, towards the end, smarter by adding conservation easements to its arsenal and proposing to sell hundreds of thousands of its acres to the Nature Conservancy for preservation. LURC at last agreed. But the houses and resorts stayed in the plans, and the jobs will come and the tax base increases and the flatlanders spend money on vacation. Among all the competing interests, this is the way the world goes, something for everyone, the art and mud of constant compromise.

One of the great outcomes of the twentieth century, achieved in part because of those who deified Thoreau, is that there is now at least the desire to make environmental rules. Yet we have many rights of property in this country, for individuals and corporations. Any kind of government, LURCing or otherwise, finds it difficult to tell us what to do with our land except when we decide to "improve" it. Then we follow the rules. But what are the rules for developing the undeveloped?

In the absence of the religious justification that drove America's settlement, where do we turn for guidance? We must preserve the wildness, yet we will develop it. What are the rights of REITS anyway? Is the ecology movement strong enough to deal with them?

Assume the answer is no, or just barely. Assume that the Plum Creeks of the world will continue to push development, and succeed as often as not. Assume that development is inevitable. Assume in the absence of anything else that government directs our moral imperatives, stepping in to force consensus and at least preserve a few treasures forever.

᳚ঌ

If belief is hopeless, we must yet continue to hope. The health of Earth and humans depends on it. The antidote to asphalt is the country lane, to quarter-pounders the wild blueberry, to soul-shredding despair the crazy loons on the lake. If the deer eat your dahlias, that only means there's still enough space for the deer. Leave the motors in Massachusetts; they are not the secret to happiness. A life of computers, or conversations, or chevrons is a life, yes, but without revelation it withers and dies.

A life (a week, a day, even an hour) in the woods does not die. It persists, in the carbon we share with the tree and the bobcat, in the poetry we share with our children. I go to the woods to feel small and insignificant—in order to feel freely at large.

In the Book of Revelation John's vision of Zion is determinedly urban, his vision of Nature cataclysmic. How about we reverse the eschatology?

Elvers

I FIRST ATE EEL SOMETIME LATE IN 1975, in a harbor-front dive on the south coast of Korea. The weather would have been wintry, and the restaurant dirty, the wooden tables worn and scored, the clientele noisy, but the views were exquisite, of fishing boats, undeveloped islands, and the aquamarine sea. By then we had a few months of kimchi and seaweed soup under our belts, as it were, and it was time to dig deeper and try the native thing, the adult thing.

It was a year of firsts for a twenty-something couple from the Midwest: flying to San Francisco and Seoul, living near the ocean, living in a city dense with poverty and xenophobia. Until 1975, fish had meant frozen fish sticks, fresh fried perch, bullheads rolled in batter. Koreans, however, were adventurous eaters, and they seemed to delight in testing the Americans. They started us that first night on simple *maki* rolls, then called for *nigiri* of tuna and shrimp and flounder and eel. We ate, timidly at first, then boldly. *Sashimi* took a little longer, maybe a second or third visit to the waterfront, and eventually I even proved my manhood by eating the almost impossibly spicy local aphrodisiac: baby octopus, freshly killed and still squirming in a bowl of red sauce.

Eel was in a way the easiest, for *unagi* is cooked before it's served. (On the other end of the scale, it took until our second year before I could eat raw oysters for breakfast.) So we passed those tests, if not many of the others posed by the culture, but at least for me sushi became more than a rite of passage or a badge of honor: it was irresistible in taste and emblematic of the exotic and the pure.

That was imperial eating; for a buck or two the innocent riches of an unpolluted sea kept on coming to our plates.

Life has calmed down somewhat since those heady days of Peace Corps forty years ago. Upon return to the US, my fortunes turned corporate, and travel became a matter more of making money than understanding culture. I have kept up with almost nothing that is Asian, save one business trip to Tokyo, occasional meals of kimchi chigae or nigiri in a restaurant, brief looks at scrolls and pots in museums, and infrequent contact with former volunteers. I have little interest in reviving memories of that time, some of them dark and thorny. It's hard to explain now why I'm thinking more and more of Korea. Perhaps in times of stress one returns to the place where innocence became experience.

I still do crave sushi, especially eel. It tastes just as good in America's clean and quiet restaurants as it did in Korea, but I suppose I should have been thinking all these recent alarming years—in my new focus on ecology and saving land—about its sustainability. But I haven't, blandly assuming that sushi magically appears from Asia, a safe reification of adventures of the past.

The news this early spring wakes me up, at least concerning eels. I've become a twice-daily website Maine-iac for news of wildness discovered and glories saved and journeys fulfilled (also the juicy depredations of human avarice). Nearly every day lately, MPBN radio and the local Penobscot Bay papers and even *The New York Times* breathlessly report on the latest hoopla up here: fishing for elvers, the little two-inch juvenile eels running up the rivers to find a home.

I'm hooked—another iconic Maine creature to write about, a new mind adventure. Some of these eels are being no less than hijacked. Their natural history is short-circuited, a new life cycle crudely managed in buckets and planes. There's a slight chance that, some months hence, the unagi I eat at Suzuki's in Rockland will not have magically appeared by some Asian sleight-of-hand. Nor will it be native except in the most twisted of senses. It may indeed have started out as an elver in a river Down East, but then humans intervened: dipped out of the river by, say, a Passamaquoddy Indian, sold to an Asian dealer (often Korean) prowling the coast, trucked live to Logan Airport in Boston, flown to Asia (again, often Korea), force-fed in a pond to the point of edibility, cooked and frozen and flown back to Logan to be trucked up to Maine for meat. It's an *Eel*-iad of unnatural proportion.

Why all the fuss about a fish one can barely see, let alone catch? Why this torturous intervention in a natural cycle?

Quite simply, money. (And sex: eels won't breed in captivity.) Eels are becoming scarce, from over-fishing, pollution, parasites, poachers and disease, the consumer demands of globalization, and warmer waters due to climate change. Governments step in with regulations, even quotas. Prices rise sharply. And then, recently, Europe banned exports and the 2011 tsunami wiped out some of the aquaculture in Japan, and the eel burst out of obscurity and into the jaws of the media. That's when international markets spectacularly reached the coast of Maine, and in its springtime rivers, burly men in camo shirts and waders, some carrying guns, set out to net elvers coming in on the tides, often in the dead of night, and sell them for $2,000 a pound, cash. In the two-month season in 2012, one guy made $700,000.

Such men seem almost a species apart from a neighborhood naturalist like me. They are exotic enough that a reality show about elver fishing, "Cold River Cash," now airs. It joins a recent raft of shows set in Maine—"Down East Dickering," "North Woods Law," "American Loggers"—in a strange new kind of nature glorification: backwoods noir.

No wonder I'm thinking about Korea. Worlds are clashing, even on the bucolic coast of Maine.

That's what it felt like in 1975, a buffeting of bodies and languages, as if my wife and I had been thrown into a city of Babel. We signed up for an adventure (and to give something back to the world, or, in other words, to escape or repudiate American values) and it turned out to be a trek that I never really understood, or liked. There were too many people in Korea, for one thing, knotted and twined on the streets by sex and age, slightly menacing in their social certainties.

Walking through cities was like swimming against a cold, dark current. It was an ancient, adult world.

In the boys' middle-school where I taught, I came to feel like one of the students, like a carefree Korean kid suddenly introduced to the rigors of examinations and uniforms and drills and corporal punishment that the culture demanded. Like them, I quickly lost most of any sense of wonder. My fellow teachers weren't much happier than their students. Their regimentation was, if possible, even worse, and their main release from it was a kind of patriotic drinking: men banded together at night around the makkoli table, lifted a bowl, and immediately were able to say virtually anything they wanted, even constructive criticisms of the government. They were "drunk" at that first sip, and the words would be forgiven, as if they never happened. This is not to say that most of the men wouldn't get hammered besides.

God knows how the women coped. Ruling their households must have been small compensation. My wife in her girls' middle school could testify that she had no outlet at all. Drinking wasn't really allowed, except with other foreigners, in other cities. She seemed more and more to crave the company of our fellow volunteers, in other cities. I was too callow to understand, and in our tiny room we read more, knitted more, wrote more, spoke together less and less. The difficulties of language and custom and public baths and outhouse toilets and loneliness became the excuse for a slow and unacknowledged drifting apart.

Thus, callow youths became seasoned adults. That first bright vividness we saw, of farmers and fishermen living on an uncorrupted coast as they had for hundreds of years, gave way to anxiety masked by tedium. We did not get close to our host family, or co-teachers. We were there to do a job, and life quickly became something to be endured until the next vacation. Or so I felt. Every few months we got out of that beautiful seaside town and traveled like any other tourists, with our American friends, to the big cities of Pusan and Seoul, to Japan, to the Hundred Island beaches of the Philippines. And after Peace Corps, we continued to trek—three months in Southeast Asia and Europe, a vacation to visit grad-school friends studying kinship on the Navajo reservation, weekends in Vermont and New Hampshire and Maine—but we could not unlearn the parsimony of reserve.

What I did learn in Korea was resolve and confidence and forbearance, but I leaned them as if they were business skills to master. They served me well, at a cost that only now am I starting to appreciate.

Like so many others, I have consumed cultures far from their points of origin; I've flown high above places to bury restlessness or to secure deals. In retirement, I've lived half-time in Maine for some years now, my own feeble migration from freshwater to salt, and I still have gotten no closer to an eel than sushi on a lacquered plate. My M.O. in communing with nature has been to take a bit of wildness, preferably one that's iconic to Maine, observe it from a distance, read about it, walk around a bit and think, look at it from a deck or granite ledge, watch a video, write about it. That's the safer way to live. But the more profound disturbances of life often occur in the deep holes of menacing memories. Those are the squirmy places we don't go. Those are the Indian reservations of shame. Those are the places where adult eels live.

American freshwater eels live the great majority of their lives, some twenty or thirty years, in lakes and ponds—mysterious, nocturnal. But then they feel the pull of the salt in their blood and they prepare for the end by what must be a glorious migration to the ocean, down rivers and streams to the seaweed beds of the eerie and heavenly Sargasso Sea, where they spawn and die. (If they make it that far, that is: the turbines of hydroelectric dams chop up their own kind of sushi.) The freshwater part of this migration has been well-documented. But the saltwater phase is almost completely unknown. Only recently have their spawning beds been identified. No one has ever even seen a freshwater eel in the ocean, let alone one spawning.

I too have felt the pull of water, since I was a teenager in fact, when my family would leave the hot plains of Minnesota for a few glorious summers in the woods and lakes and trout streams of northern Michigan. But I didn't get back to such places for a long time, except as a vacationer, a consumer. The trials and joys of the adult life intervened: the trials of making a career, the joys of raising a family. My own release from stress was always the dream of the North Country, especially the coast of Maine. I wanted intimate knowledge of rocks and deer and the delirious battering sea of a place that would be home, where one's very bones could say anything they wanted. And it's coming almost entirely true. The business travel ended, and Yeats's famous gyre isn't widening but narrowing, the center has had a chance to hold. One eventually finds one's place, and how wonderful to have the privilege to contemplate such beauty at leisure, inhabit it, and write about it.

No wonder I'm thinking more about Koreans—my sense of place is still so tenuous and theirs isn't. Their tradition and culture demand loyalty. And what did I carry back to America? Not much more than an ordeal manfully and gainfully endured, some deep, now rumbling disquiet, and the preciousness of raw fish. At the sushi bar I always save the two pieces of unagi for last, after the rolls and the salmon and the shrimp and the yellowtail. Eel flesh is soft and satisfying, roasted in a sweet and salty sauce, bound to vinegary rice by a thin strip of nori, bound in my mind to a more colorful and ingenuous time. Like an imperialist, I took only what I wanted then. And now: of course we shouldn't be eating any fish served as sushi, they're all endangered, on all the red lists. But we do. Memory and pleasure, however guilty, are stronger than responsibility. We citizens of the global village, we businessmen, rationalize like crazy. Somehow we deserve such things, the reward for cooptation by the life cycle of capitalism. If we don't consume, someone else will.

∾

In this tangled web of memory and desire, there are other migrants besides elvers and businessmen. Thousands of years ago, Asians crossed the Bering land bridge into North America and became American Indians. Like most things on the continent, their lives of hunting and fishing (including eeling) and farming were completely changed by the European influx. The Passamaquoddy of Maine, for example, are now penned in a reservation in the farthest northeast corner of the US, in the poorest county in Maine and nearly the poorest in the country. Their fishermen and hunters are pale shadows, a desperate echo, of what used to be, their licenses and quotas for wildlife, including elvers, granted by the state and the feds in a kind of mocking tribute to the abundance of the past. Nobody much cared when elvers were selling for $35 a pound. But when the price jumped sixty-fold, the tribe saw a way to jump-start its people out of poverty. It started issuing its own licenses, claiming sovereign status and the ability to manage its own fishery, a little something beyond permission to stage bingo, and the state had to disagree, and police in 4x4s descended to break up the rebellion.

Today's Native Americans, I suspect, would fish out the resource as quickly as anyone else, especially at these prices—"Nothing dollarable is safe," John Muir said—or maybe they wouldn't. Maybe such deep connections to the land would make a difference. What would it be like to see generations of your ancestors all around, to see the spirits of Manitou in every deer and rock? Now that's the kind of reality show we really need.

No wonder I'm thinking more and more about Korea. I'm growing older, and what binds Native Americans and Koreans together besides genes is that they respect the elderly. (Or should I ask, is America the only country in the world that does not?) At the age of 60, Koreans suddenly achieve a kind of social perfection and become wise, pampered by their families, and not a little imperial. I can't imagine the transformation, having little sense of generational belonging. But the smells and the tastes of the place come back strongly now, the sense of discovery, the assaults and parries, the difficult nights of unspoken strife, sublimated stress. What are the memories trying to say? Maybe I became an adult not in spite of the foreignness of Asia, but because of it. A place so hard to live in, so antithetical to the quiet way I was raised, was the rudest of introductions to adulthood. I had to face the difficulties and overcome them, and that training has proved useful in adult life, in navigating corporate pollution, in managing disillusionment and divorce. I learned, in effect, to be a good Confucian and process the squirmiest of stuff into the emblems of culture. Yet somehow the dreams of youth, like the pull of the sea, stayed true. I remember places, not itineraries.

Now that I'm in my sixties, maybe the last decades of a life can be as sensory as the pure air and rushing trout streams of my teens, as the sushi joints and jostling streets and packed local buses of my twenties. I'll need to face some truths, however. I can't keep claiming that the past is not important, that one can pick and choose among experiences. Maybe I faked being an adult. I claim that my divorce was amicable and easy, no kids, few possessions, but of course it couldn't have been, she must have been terribly hurt. I claim that my second life is a wonderful one, and it is, but has it been too comfortable, and have I kept wife and daughters and friends at some kind of emotional distance, and therefore failed to feel the full force of love?

In a few more years, certainly by the end of my life, the elver craze will be over. Eels will be extirpated, or scientists will learn to breed them in captivity, or gourmands will plunder another exotic consumable. In ecology, as perhaps elsewhere, the rare thing loses and the commonplace wins, and the winners are often, ironically, invasives from Asia like kudzu, green crabs, knotweed, ash borers, eel parasites, bamboo. Right in front of me, however, the elemental sea remains, as yet un-murdered, full of treasures and mystery, and many rivers still run deep and cold, and the waters tell me, if I'd only listen, to stop composing life to my liking, get off my deck every once in a while, and make a journey to my own Sargasso Sea, perhaps untangling these memories in a book, perhaps running the rapids of the Allagash, looking for the undiscoverable eel.

Human Natures

THE WORKSHOP ON COMMUNITY CONSERVATION is coming to a close, and the facilitator, perhaps anticipating a flagging audience after a long day, moves to a contemplative moment in her agenda. "Take a few quiet moments to think about people and land," she says, "then write a statement that begins with the words 'I believe' and share it with a colleague." For many in the room, the exercise is hard. They are land-trust executive directors prone to hiding personal revelations, or they're taciturn native Mainers, or people of action rather than words, or, in several cases, all three. For me, it is much easier. I am none of these, and what's more, I was raised a Calvinist, well used to statements of the leap of faith.

Behind our facilitator's challenge is a current rage—telling stories out loud—and not just for entertainment via podcast. There has come to be a political angle. We know now that persuading someone to believe something has much greater impact if the propaganda is couched in a personal narrative. People respond to the arc of drama, to sincerity and empathy. A story about one's own cancer, or a sister's abortion, or in our case, about a restorative hour on a mountain top, has a much greater chance of changing minds than a pamphlet or a preachment. We are encouraged to use stories and their cousins-in-law, beliefs, hopes, and dreams.

That's because many of us Baby Boomers in the land-trust movement are being asked to change our tunes, even though our generation has been the catalyst for tremendous growth. The movement's venerable roots in Massachusetts in 1891 notwithstanding, the perpetual protection of land had its real growth, a re-birth almost, in the 1970s and 80s. After the Vietnam War we turned downward as much as inward. Our idealism found legacy in the ground. We worked on property owners to give land, and we worked on donors to give money, all of this conducted passionately like a religion. We've succeeded to the tune of millions of acres, and a biota of trillions therefore still sings its ancient, antiphonal choruses.

But now we've reached a kind of institutional adolescence, and we're flagellating ourselves like teenagers. Is saving the wilderness enough of a mission? What happens when it runs out? Isn't preserving trees just a gesture toward climate change, not a cure, not on the scale we need? What do we do about people? Can we change their minds, their baser instincts? We worry that we are seen as elitist, that we take land away from people and tax rolls and hide it away, that wildness trumps every human concern. How are we going to succeed with the next generations, who may well try to re-define the whole idea of perpetuity, if we can't engage them on their terms?

These questions are disruptive for many, including me. I'm a land guy first and foremost, a nineteenth century transcendental-romantic wannabe. "Keep 'em out," I mutter. "The earth is beseeching us to survive." There are a lot of us, preservers of the pure, barriers to the new. We suffer the status-quo bias. We're convenient conservatives. Don't change a thing in the woods or on the shore, we say, something we'd be ashamed to say regarding marriage equality, and money in politics, and income disparity. Hence, the workshop on change, hence the articulation of beliefs. And hence my fall-back on human natures, the Calvinistic and dualistic war within us.

What belief statement do I write down in that workshop? Something like this: "I believe that people always screw up nature. Yet I also believe everyone can experience joy in nature, as I do, even for a moment." I go on to admit out loud to my colleagues that I can't stand the noise of a pack of rowdy hikers on a mountain top. I admit out loud that they must be allowed there, encouraged to be there, if there's any hope for the world.

This fight is the essence, and the curse, of Calvinism. Not for the first time my training in absurdity and contradiction comes in handy. Countless sermons and catechism classes and Sunday school homilies tried to teach me that we have original sin from birth, that each person's fate is predestined, that only belief can save humankind. (If you can get your mind around that unholy trinity, see me after class. [Yes, I'm preaching a doctrine, not telling a story.]) This means, among other crazy things, that good deeds are powerless to save us. Yet, and but, and however: I know in my heart (and in catechism: this is the great and perhaps only lesson I took from nineteen years of indoctrination) that the only way to conquer despair is to act in hope, as if doing good deeds could indeed save us. Our human natures compel us to be righteous even as they drive us to extinction.

There's a reason that the Bible is divided into Old and New Testaments. For all its brutality and cynicism and mind-numbing lists of obligations and restrictions, the Old Testament is essentially a book of stories. That these stories, of creation and floods and whales and exoduses and wars, were derived not just from the Hebrew God but from thousands of years of other cultures as well is the best part, the human part. In the New Testament, a different God appears, the preachy kind, the kind that pushes on you for salvation. And that's part of human nature too, the need to hope and believe in a better life.

If these two parts of us are inevitably true (the one part, the destructive part, for sure, and the other? Still a leap of faith for most, I'm afraid.), then what does that mean for land trusts? It means we must work to save Nature from humans, even as we provide places for them to trash it. It means that places of wilderness without humans are free of original sin. It means we must preserve wild places for as long as possible, which qualification in itself implies that the possible won't last forever. And so I believe we need to serve both sides, status quo and change, solitude and society, rest and adventure, endangered leatherback and inner-city child, and in those moments of joy, bring them together. When God has left the building, what do we have left?

In my own land trust, there is a taste of wilderness left. There are plenty of preserved places in the hills and valleys and fields and woods where you can be alone, at least for a while (alas, that's very hard to accomplish on lakefront or ocean shore, which have long since been claimed by the well-to-do). That's important, to have the promise of solitude and inspiration practically on your doorstep.

But there is no old-growth forest left here in mid-coast Maine, no unexplored cove. Every hill has been logged several times. I daresay, in 10,000 years of habitation, every inch has felt a human foot. Our trust's lands are open to walking and hiking, hunting and biking. We preserve one bald coastal hill mostly for human use, a stone hut at its top offering both long, blue vistas and community events celebrating poetry and art and solstices and full moons and blueberry picks and kids flying kites on a magical afternoon. Beech Hill is no wilderness, but it's inspiring, and even necessary.

But we're being asked to go further. Land-trust folks are becoming developers not of housing estates and shopping malls but of community health and well-being. We work with juvenile offenders to do trail work in lieu of jail time. We run farmer's markets. We are sustainable foresters and organic farmers, and we provide safe harbors for fishermen. We dream of solar farms on our land, tidal turbines just offshore. We work with political refugees, inner-city kids, migrants, the infirm. We believe this is right. People must benefit from the land even as we preserve it. This is the best way to ensure perpetuity, if the forest is truly a community treasure for contemplation, regeneration, re-birth.

But I'm going to submit that community involvement is not enough. Land (and sea) is not just a vast therapist's couch. We crave wild land. Wildness is a mother, the original gene pool. We attempt to co-opt wild experience—RVs, zip lines, parasailing, glam-camping—at our peril; Mother Nature sees right through these propitiations. Only in preserving and feeling wilderness are we stating that we understand the worst of human nature, and embrace it.

Even on my land trust's well-used preserves, I get a strong sense not only of what used to be, but also of what still exists elsewhere. Just a few miles to my north is Maine's Great North Woods, 3.5 million acres used for logging, recreation, and, in some places still, almost perfect isolation. Farther north are the vast untouched boreal forests of Canada, the mountains of Alaska, the frozen bounties of the Arctic. Pure rain forest still exists in South America, Africa, bits of Southeast Asia, even Puerto Rico. Knowing this is important to the health of our species. We are built to dream on land, to believe in wildness, and therefore to accept death.

Watching vultures soaring in the thermals, osprey diving in the coves, eagles raiding a nest—this is what I live for. They kill, and fly, and die, and I accept my own arc. And when the last evidence of them is a NOVA documentary, then the two natures of being human will hardly matter anymore. We too will be images on a screen, brains only. We will have no roots or guts. Contradictions will be banned from belief. Even now we think the good life, even eternal life, is within the grasp of our digital talons, even as we burn one hundred fifty acres of rain forest every minute of every day.

How desperately important it is, then, to bring together people and nature, to take a kid to a vernal pool deep in the woods where she learns what a frog is and must be, let alone how it feels to hold one in her hand, in her wild, untamed, and mortal heart.

Moss and Lichen

THE NORTH SIDE OF THE GARAGE ROOF is getting green, so you decide to do something about it. Strictly amateur—no new-age zinc strips or cleansing vinegar washes. It will be boring work, on a hot day, but even the nastiest of tasks—clipping grass around the base of the deck where the mosquitoes swarm, for example, or pulling prickly beach-rose runners out of the garden—are not so bad here in Maine.

Of course once you get started, you can't stop. Climb up the ladder, scrape as far as hand can reach and muscles can take, switch to your left hand, scrape some more; climb down the ladder and move it over a few feet; repeat. Moss is pliable stuff, easy-going, basically useless, and the Japanese like it in gardens (calm-, still-, timeless- and other nesses), and it looks most picturesque on rocks and trees in the woods, and that's about it.

Besides the moss, there are patches of lichen on the roof, and lichen is a much different beast. Extremely slow-growing and tough, lichens colonize algae in order to live and have been called fungi that discovered agriculture. There are two kinds here: the kind that's grey-green and flaky and the kind that's whitish or reddish and almost irretrievably integrated with the crushed stone skin of the shingles. You hack away anyway. This is surely shortening the life of the roof, you think later. The roofer you eventually have to hire will gaze at you with the puzzled look that Mainers tend to give flatlanders.

You're called to dinner and it takes a lot of willpower to stop the scraping. Just one more patch, soft and green, clinging to the asphalt shingles with a thousand little feet, peeled off in satisfying clumps, then you'll go in and commune with your family.

You finish the north side the next morning, right after the second cup of coffee and a couple of chapters of Russell Banks. Once you remove everything that's reachable (for a brief and foolish moment you think *I could just ease off the ladder, cling to the roof and get that moss up top, no problem*, but you're not twenty anymore and the roof is steep), you move the ladder around to the south side, where there's almost no moss and only a few bits of lichen. No matter, they have to go.

And now, since you've gone to all the trouble of the ladder and the muscles, there's the house itself, even though the roof faces east/west (except for the addition in front), so it doesn't have moss and only a few patches of lichen and doesn't need this therapy. After another day of such behavior, you stop only when you get to the edge of the addition and the hornets under the eave start to protest. One or two are mad enough to sting. Well, the last couple of days weren't really about clean roofs anyway. Moss and lichens, you slow and useless beings, we need to recruit you for the twenty-first century.

⁂

There has been a spate of writing lately about the horrors of the present computer age—the decline of reading, the pace of life, the intrusion of technology. It seems we can't exist without pixel fixes. It might be simple paranoia; we have to know at all times what's happening so it doesn't creep up on us. It might be micro-boredom, the ability to stop thinking after a minute or two. It might be pure addiction, what Edward Hallowell in *CrazyBusy* calls screen sucking.

Or is it that screens, like lichen, have discovered agriculture? Given enough symbiosis and the picked-up pace of evolution, I say we'll be seeing new varieties of humans in just a few thousand years.

Pixels will be embedded directly in skin, and it will be quite unclear who's doing the sucking.

One type of human already exhibits many of these mutations. Home for the holidays, certain college students sit in your living room in Massachusetts and simultaneously use the phone (voice, voice mail, text) and the computer (email, Facebook, YouTube), and talk to you their parents as well—who feel proud to have evolved as far as email.

Email is so last year, the changelings say. You sort of have to try to be formal with spelling and proper grammatical construction, whatever, and it takes so long to arrive.

But parties of the other certain age need to be bored. We get tired just thinking about Apple apps. We actually come to Maine to be boring. So please, peoples of the world, do your bit to stave off the further evolution of humans—kick back and watch the moss re-grow on the roof of your garage. In another few years you can scrape it again.

From the Mountaintop

TWO YOUNG MARRIEDS talk on their 'droids at the top of Beech
Hill in Maine. They are directing the delivery of pencil-liner
tiles for their new master bathroom in Virginia, and without
hesitation they place and answer calls from sister and mother back
home, their pinch-hitters in the coordination of men and material.
We listen in.

Nick looks up from his phone. "I can't get hold of Eddie. He's not
answering."

Jess says, "I'll call Mom."

"Mom? We can't find Eddie. So just leave the key for him under
the back tire of the Prius."

Pause.

"The left back tire."

Pause.

"As you face the car from the back."

Pause.

"No, we do it all the time. It'll be OK."

They put their phones away and look around again at the coast
of Maine.

Now, Beech Hill is one of the most beautiful places on the coast, a
rare bald hill with 360-degree views of land and water, of the Camden
Hills behind, of the mystical islands of Penobscot Bay before, of the

ocean beyond. Organic blueberry fields carpet the hillsides, and the hill itself is topped by a gentleman's retreat from a hundred years ago, built of stone, recently restored, wild flowers growing out of its sod roof. Even after many visits here I stand dumbstruck by the view. Today I should be dumbstruck by desecration. Who would carry a phone up here, much less use it? How do people even manage it? And so competently too, no slobbering or stuttering, no trying to talk with your mouth hanging open in wonder. Normal speech is difficult enough in this place of quiet and wind and hallucinations of salvation. I can hardly get words out to you when we're here alone. And you're my wife. Speech would be impossible on a phone. What kinds of people contemplate their master bath up here?

Today, however, my inner ire is a bit complicated. The couple is my nephew and his wife, on vacation, visiting us. Doubly dumbstruck, I can't say anything or even mutter dark imprecations. Those tiles are related to me.

I try to catch your eye, to see what you're thinking. Rolling eyeballs? Amused tolerance? But you don't care to play, or won't, you're busy with how to capture, in the lens of your camera, the sky and fields reflecting in the windows of another time.

So let me grumble to myself for a minute. How the world seems so self-absorbed, self-referential, selfish. How the screens rule, the dumb phones, the smart phones, the netbooks, the tablets, the laptops, the desktops, the TV, the home theaters, the movie theaters. How future devices will not bother with Off buttons. How we will wear our computers like shirts. How our heads will swell, our bodies atrophy. How the present generation is going to hell in a hand-held.

And definitely how mountaintops aren't what they used to be: not sacred, not awe-inspiring, not the home of gurus or the metaphor of a king. Now 5,000 people climb Everest every year, and helicopters blithely drop skiers in the high Rockies as if no amount of snow or altitude or expense could pose a barrier to pleasure. It's a world in which "every mountain and hill shall be made low," a world in which the Bible, so quoted on a website from West Virginia, justifies mountaintop removal for coal.

I get myself steamed up a little, and I want to ask my nephew how he does it. He's standing here on the edge of heaven, talking on the phone again. "Hey, Eddie, it's Nick. The key is under the back tire of the Prius. Call me back when you get in the house."

But I don't dare to intrude. I'm of a generation that thinks its metaphors should apply to everyone, and I don't care just now, here on Beech Hill, to have the theory tested. Maybe we'll talk about it at dinner, back among our routers and our sofas.

You and I, we've talked about these things in the privacy of our own dinner table. We worry about the "younger generation," their social world narrowing even as the virtual world expands. It can't be good, all this immediacy and all this distance. You can't feel human without the glances of a flirt, the glinting of an ocean wave. Edward Abbey said, "Life is already too short to waste on speed," and "To be everywhere at once is to be nowhere forever." And he didn't have computers. We shake our heads like old people, and then you laugh, pointing out that we ourselves are plunked most of the day in front of a screen, working or writing (or pretending to), and many evenings in front of a TV, recuperating (or pretending to). "Besides," you say, "you yourself love nothing more than to get away from people."

I eat my pique and join the others on the porch of the house. Another young couple sits in the shade, unpacking lunch out of a backpack; their baby sucks on a bottle. My nephew says, "What a cutie-pie," and the baby's mother thanks him in a German accent. Nick is wonderful with people. I watch him talk and gaze, joke and contemplate. He was born at the tail end of the 1970s and didn't experience, like his father and I did, the day of the longhairs, the dreams of a generation. Instead, he suffered Ronald Reagan, raging consumerism, 9/11, unfunded and undeclared wars, and more financial booms and busts than a body should endure. No wonder he keeps his own counsel, no wonder his mountaintop is a matter of fact, not fiction. And no wonder, maybe, his determination.

The lesson of the 'droid says so. The new man doesn't buy this journey-versus-goal stuff. He doesn't climb to reach the top, he just climbs, because the top is much the same as the climb, everything streaming all around him, all the time, integrated in time, waiting to be plucked: tiles out of the air, friendship out of a screen, a good life out of Tyson's Corner, always connected. He doesn't need to save the world, he is the world. He doesn't have to choose so dramatically, between Vietnam and Canada, between the wildflower and the bull-dozer, between love and war. Has he achieved what we hoped?

Things are different, that's for sure. It's as if the world is flat again. Certainly, it is completely and safely navigable: a GPS screen both defines and defeats adventure. A lot of folks don't want the unpredict-able crevice or the weird yeti or the dangerous excitement of almost falling off the edge. Folks want fences.

Our "older" generation seems worried about this. We like met-aphor, and metaphor might lose its power when facts stain the air, when a constellation, a quote from a sage, or the name, history, population, and house prices of that island shimmering in the bay all sit in the device in one's hand. We're haunted by the 1960s when it was us versus them, and we had to keep the faith, for what it was worth. We tried to follow Thoreau when he said, far ahead of any-one else, "The tops of mountains are among the unfinished parts of the globe, whither it is a slight insult to the gods to climb and pry into their secrets, and try their effect on our humanity. Only daring and insolent men, perchance, go there." We thought we were daring and insolent, eagerly climbing our mountains like Thoreau did Katahdin, gleefully offering our slight insults to the gods. It was OK; God or the gods had left the globe and we were dying to replace them.

Did we? Some of us are still taking to the tops of hills (just hills now, we're too old to attempt Mt. Katahdin or its like). It is still a pilgrimage, slightly attenuated for better or worse. Up high I for one pretend that the rest of the world doesn't matter, that my metaphoric gods can save me from it. It's clean, and usually quiet, and what one can see of civilization is far off. Hawks pray in the thermals, blue-berries burst like sacramental wine on the tongue, and you and I sit on pews of granite, holding hands. That sounds as if we left no gods behind, just replaced them. And often it's enough.

But more and more often the journey up is hard, making our knees sore, our necks sweat, more and more we have to come to grips with mortality (a difficult concept for Boomers), and sometimes we learn that the goal is both the trek and the mountaintop, that we get closer to the infinite by honest perspiration . . . and for a moment I don't worry about by dividing things up so neatly. I'm up on Beech Hill, and if the ether streams news and porn and recipes and tweets and suggestions for interior decoration, fine—I can leave them for others to believe.

Except I still worry about the children. What kind of world will that little German baby find when he grows up? He'll be world-savvy, but also maybe world-weary.

Nick and I stand side by side, mumbling pleasantries into the blue. I don't think we have to make sense, or actually say the words that redeem and save. I'm confident he won't ignore the cell tower in a forest, a hundred turbines on a ridgeline, a mountain leveled for coal, an end to the ends of the earth. For now, for us, the glory of the view is enough. Last night, in the clear country air, we went out to see the stars and he pointed his phone at the heavens, and constellations appeared on his screen, named in Greek, stars connected. He grinned in pleasure, you and I crowed in disbelieving delight.

And when, in a few minutes, we go back to earth and the parking lot, his devices will warn and my tropes will inspire, and the memory of the magnificence of bay and mountains and stars will pierce both our hearts even unto Tyson's Corner. That lesson again for us fogies? Preach less. Absorb more.

We walk down Beech Hill. Nick and Jess gradually move ahead, until they're out of earshot. I think about making a remark to you about phones and views, but shut up. You will rightly point out to me that Nick and Jess are more grounded than us old dreamers, in better shape to tackle the world, and that our own daughters, half a generation behind them, are the same. You will sense, of course, that that's my real worry, my daughters' future.

What have we passed on to them? What kind of world? What kind of morals? Their phones are always buzzing, they speak a kind of pop-culture patois between them that drives me mad, their friend-ships seem as important as philosophy, and yet I know, as surely as I know my love for two little girls in pajamas "reading" *Goodnight Moon* in my lap, for two pre-teens negotiating the dangers of middle school, for two elegant young women braving athletics and scholas-tics and heuristics, yet I surely know that they have a chance at the best of both worlds. Not through a religious prism: as parents we have eschewed that, and they haven't been curious. But through a moral one, featuring a facility with both society and nature.

That knowledge helps the dread in my gut that their every set-back, every rejection by college or lover or friend or job, is a kick in my romantic view of life. It medicates the acid I sometimes feel for the way my generation has turned idealism into consumerism.

At dinner tonight, over a bottle of the cab franc they brought north from their favorite Virginia vineyard, I might still ask Nick and Jess how they deal, how the torch can be passed, will they bring children into this world. At the end of the evening, especially if they've had a few glasses, they might very well say something like: "It's a new world, get over yourself. Mountaintops aren't what they used to be. It's a fact of life that the snows of Kilimanjaro will melt. A wind turbine on a high ridge may be as beautiful as a conifer. The twenty-first century doesn't need Martin Luther King, Jr., and that Ten Commandments and Moses thing? That's so tribal. We'll deal. And so will our kids."

I don't think that will be their answer, but if it is, I will look at their resolve, and trust them as if they were my own children, and try my best to believe what they say.

Loon

O N THE LAST DAY OF THE YEAR, at dawn on a ten-degree morning, a man lies in bed thinking about *temps perdu*. Just offshore, a loon yodels, announcing itself and its territory as if summer never left.

As usual, the man's family is celebrating anti-New Year's Eve in Maine. The drive north on the thirtieth has been made, salmon from Jess's Market broiled for dinner, a quiet night passed, and now anticipation grows for a morning of reading books and staring at sea smoke on the bay, a walk later to Ash Point, an early dinner at a favorite restaurant from the kids' childhood, a movie on Netflix, bed by ten. No fireworks, stupid hats, dropping balls, champagne, headaches, waste. No temptation to fiddle while Rome burns or party like there's no tomorrow. What's to celebrate? Another year to be claimed as the hottest on record? More consumption ahead? Well, OK, there is that slight temptation to say the hell with the quiet life. Carouse, spend, drive fast, turn up the heat. Bad news can make you reckless.

He turns over and looks out to sea. His inner sybarite fades away. The loon calls again: let's stay in the north forever.

When he thinks about loons, he thinks about fragility. A third of the males die in mating season in fights over territory. Once fertile, a mated pair makes a ridiculous nest of grass and twigs on the edge of the shore, in full view of predators. Loons can hardly walk on land, hence the derivation of "loon" from Old English for lummox. Innocently, they eat lead sinkers, mistaking them for gastroliths to aid their digestion. They've been thought to be funny, crazy, eerie. Motor-heads in power boats try to run them down. Loons from the lakes of the Midwest and inland Canada sensibly migrate to the Gulf of Mexico for the winter, but the ones from the lakes of Maine are apparently dyslexic and fly to the icy coves of the Gulf of Maine. The Canadian dollar coin is called the loonie not only because the loon is featured on the reverse but because Canadians don't take themselves too seriously, and the name used to seem vaguely funny, or at least self-deprecating. Now Canada mines tar sands for oil and cuts boreal forests for toilet paper and no loon is laughing.

There's nothing funny in nature except what humans bring to it. We photograph animals in hats, in laundry baskets, kissing under mistletoe, doing the things we wish we could, as if we were innocent of the burden of time. In nature time merely passes. Humans are the only animals that squander it.

Are we squandering it? The man puts a human trait to work, his memory. A few months before, he and his wife and daughter and her boyfriend canoed a lake in central Maine on a late September day. The lake had a camp and nothing else on its shores but trees and rocks. Mt. Katahdin filled the view to the north. The day was bright and warm, promising a clear, cool evening. A loon surfaced close to the canoes, sleek, graceful, painted black and white in patterns like Vermeer's, perfectly within its element. It started calling. Its wail was the classic one so familiar on pure northern lakes, signaling its location for a mate, haunting like a conscience. The call reverberated around the lakeshore and in the hearts and bones of the humans.

Lying in bed, looking out on the cold bay, the man knows that is the way time should be felt: in the sun-bound rhythms of the day, in the deep-seated magic of the seasons. People and their crafts are of no account at that moment on the lake. He wonders if the loon cry could be the song at the new year, the auld lang syne, his meme of lost time. Isn't this how all of our passages should be reckoned?

Silly man: a bird's cry will never replace noisemakers, or chain saws. Now who's the crazy one?

Elements of the Allagash

S OMETHING ANCIENT AND ALCHEMICAL HAPPENS on a wilderness waterway. What we call news disappears. The word "media" sounds more like a song than a klaxon. Our bodies bask and bend, and minds follow. A pure, universal solvent dissolves facts and transmutes elements. In spruce and eagle we sense our wild genetic roots. Water and air and rock concoct a rapids, an elixir to drink in at dusk.

The best transcendence? We do not seek or preach perfection. It merely happens.

EARTH

It takes three hours to find our philosopher's stone. At 6:30 a.m., shivering in the air of early September, we're ready to go, to leave our solid town-flesh behind. We've piled our gear into a muddy pickup and are carried into the woods, bouncing over ruts and wash-outs. The driver, affable by Maine standards, answers questions but volunteers little. Conversation stumbles, halts. Logging trucks thicken the air with dust. In the middle of nowhere, a traffic jam appears: we are stopped by a backhoe covering a culvert with sharp, black pieces of slate. We can't yet imagine making gold out of this.

At last we reach the river's edge. Unloaded, our stuff lies in heaps of metal and plastic and fabric. We lade the canoes and they groan, heavy as oxen, and we get in and try to push off, and the bottoms scrape horribly on the pebbles of the shore. We stop for a moment, reluctant to lose the earth's embrace. The driver leaves, perhaps smiling.

But then we take deep breaths and go, melting into water, moving smoothly and quietly, and the only carbon we burn is our own. There are no harsh sounds of industry, just the swish of paddles, and we exult. We have slipped the surly bonds. The way north, downstream, shines in the sun.

Yet we are neophyte gliders, we three, father, daughter, daughter's friend. In the rapids we don't slide over or around rocks, we scrape them, bang them, leave paint on their crowns. It will take a day or two to outwit physics and float free. More than once, the elder of us, paddling solo, runs a riffle backwards or is pinned athwart a granite crag, stuck and mortally chagrined.

A hard, crashing diagnosis, like running into a rock, caused this gift of a trip. A solid tumor in the prostate had grown; bad cells threatened to leak into lymph and blood. The operation (steel cutting, laser burning, hope flowering) was followed by Christmas, and under the tree the daughter placed a present, a book on the Allagash and a map of wilderness. It can't be said that alchemy stopped the cells from slipping their bonds (a surgeon and his robot did that), but certainly now, in late summer, water and trees and sky complete the healing.

Each evening we return to land. The hardness of ground feels softer now, cushioned by grasses. We are lighter, stronger. Packs lose weight (or we gain muscle). Tent pegs easily push in. A backless bench is as comfortable as a La-Z-Boy. Our heaviest gear, the sleeping pads, uncoil and self-inflate, like magic.

Every afternoon, between setting up camp and cooking dinner, the celebrant hangs a hammock and suspends himself between heaven and earth.

WATER

In the rapids, air whitens the water. At first, we try to conquer currents, fighting for safe passage among brigades of stone. Then we learn to read the water, looking for Vs that show channels, following a trail of bubbles along the path of least resistance. The canoes are no longer vectors, straight and sharp. They slip and slide like otters.

A moose grazes in the river grasses. She moves slowly along the banks, well aware of the humans and not giving a damn. She has lived here for thousands of years, she will never be tamed, no rough beast will ever ride her out of water and into war.

Time is water flowing. Several times the first day we play the game of time, try to pin it down. Closest guesser by our one watch wins first prize, whoops in triumph. By day two, thanks to re-acquaintance with slants of light and growls of stomach, we predict with great accuracy, and the cheering dies off. The conventions of civilization fade like newsprint in the sun, and the river carries us on.

Time expands, or collapses, we don't know which. Which way is time running?

We wake one morning and water beads and runs down tent walls, inside and out, and sleeping bags are moist, and skin feels soft. On the river again, we can see only a few yards ahead. Water in air has overtaken our world. The future is obscured, and who cares? We put faith in our deltoids, our synapses, and the embrace of the river. Where we've been is the same as where we're going.

Air

In the wilderness we air breathers actually think about air. There's fog and cloud, and a silver maple rustling, and an eagle flying on billows, and perfumed molecules of pine, and a strong gust pushing one of us helplessly off course. Air is purely given, purely taken.

And that's about all we think about. Whole days pass without intellectual content, no one thinking of money or books, performance or prosody. (Such things, like over-thinking left-right steering problems in a canoe, only get you up a bank.) We are body-concentrating on water and air: watching the current, scouting for rocks, gazing at trees, hoping for moose, unloading canoes, soaking up sun, deep-breathing.

We do not dwell on the past. There's no thought of the past at all except the deepest of pasts, our own wild genes so obvious everywhere we look.

No one analyzes the present. No one thinks, how am I coping, am I happy or sad, what's the meaning of meaning; it is all feeling, of cool water splashed by a canoe or dipped by a hand, of warm sun on bare legs, of the taste of bacon and eggs intensified in the clean air. Even at night, in some hours of wakefulness, we look for stars or clouds, not the read-outs of clocks; hear rustlings, not sirens; feel contentment, not redress; smell pine tar and river mud, not exhaust from the interstate; touch the fabric of a tent and not a bottle of antacids.

And there is no obsession on the future, except the exciting prediction of rapids and shoals.

We think, of course, but hardly in the normal way. Normal thought makes the body seem weak, burdensome. Not here. The coordination between mind and body is seamless. The wide, wild river makes sure, its ripples and riffles and eddies and rapids demanding attention, its deep parts opening to slow, strong paddling, its rocks, hidden and seen, calling to us constantly to miss them.

The highest thought, here and everywhere, should be a paean to the elements.

FIRE

In the morning, the little propane stove burns blue as the sky, boiling the river water, which scalds the coffee grounds, which perfume the air. In the afternoon, the sun is the best of radiators. In the evening we light a campfire and roast our meat and warm our hands in the sudden chill and sit talking of quiet things in the heart, even though the fire's heart is violent plasma, fusing earth and air, snapping and shedding sparks, white and orange and red. Yet it is the calmest thing imaginable, like exploding stars twinkling in the night. Those little sparks shoot off into darkness, and we comfort ourselves in insignificance.

QUINTESSENCE

Most ancient thinkers added a fifth element to the essence of nature. This is the one you feel on the river but reason out only after you leave the river behind. It's the one that gets you into trouble, the theology that should be left out of this cosmology.

Back in your regular life, in your analytical hours, you think there has to be some meaning beyond moose and love and riffles and bacon. You despair over the infamy of war, the malice of cancer. "Oh God," (maybe even said literally), "where is the justice?" And then it gets worse. You wonder if some Big Bang or Big Baker cooked all this, if there was a definite beginning, and if there was a start, will there be an end?

It does seem so. These days of soil depleted and air polluted and seas rising and forests burning seem like the last gasp of the Anthropocene. The four elements of Nature are turning into sermons, into the four horsemen of the Apocalypse, like avatars clouding our suns and ghosting our selfies.

An Allagash of one's own gives different evidence. "Life is explained not by humans but by itself," it says. "Remember me when time gets jagged and good works despair. Jump in, float for a while, rejoice. Here you are the picture of health."

Acknowledgments

Thanks to two amazing editors, my wife Cynthia Dockrell, who muscled these essays into submission for journal publication, and copy-editor Rose Alexandre-Leach, who shaped them beautifully for book publication, and to my two amazing daughters, Kate and Emma, who suffered shore-wanderings and wool-gatherings and survived. Emma also made the line drawings that grace this book.

Thanks also to the following journals and magazines for publishing these essays in the first place. Note that many have been edited to work together in book form.

Berries	*Louisville Review* Vol. 68, October 2010
Blueberry Hill	*Emrys Journal* 31, May 2014
Pointed Firs	*Blueline* 31, May 2010
Felling Trees	*Southeast Review* 29:1, February 2011
Rockweed	*Full Grown People*, May 2014
Beyond Ash Point	*Maine Review* 3, March 2015
Yellow Finches	*Contrary* Summer, July 2009
Almost Heaven	*Eclectica* Vol. 13 No 4, October 2009
Maine Mundane	*Sangam* #1, March 2009
Tea Bags from Shaw's	*Scintilla* #3, December 2012
How to___ a ___ Lobster____	*Pank* 7:6, June 2012
Tourist	*Street Light* 10, Summer 2014
Crabs	*North Dakota Quarterly* 76:4, Fall 2009

Backward Flow	*Ampersand Review* Vol. 6, March 2011
Consider the Moose	*Gargoyle* #60, Summer 2013
With Thoreau in Maine	*Saranac Review* Issue 5, August 2009
Deer	*Devil's Lake* 11, June 15, 2015
Walking on Ash Point	*Amarillo Bay* Vol. 11 No. 2, May 2009
Bald Eagles	*Meat for Tea* 7:4, December 2013
White and Black	*Prime Number* 5, Jan 2011
Rocks and Stone	*Read This* Vol. 4, Issue 2, April 2009
Walmart on the Weskeag	*Wilderness House Literary Review* 8:3, October 2013
Trash	*Compose,* Spring 2014
Average Fuel	*Ducts* 33, Summer 2014
Lupine	*Cantaraville* Issue 9, January 2010
Revelations in the Maine Woods	*Cactus Heart* Issue 2, September 2012
Elvers	*Slice* 16 Spring/Summer, March 2015
Human Natures	not yet published
Moss and Lichen	*The Puckerbrush Review*, Vol. 27, No. 2, August 2012
From the Mountaintop	*Southern Indiana Review* 18:1, Spring 2011
Loon	*Switchback* 22, November 2015
Elements of the Allagash	*Compose,* Spring 2017

ABOUT THE AUTHOR

JIM KROSSCHELL divides his time between Owls Head, Maine and Newton, Massachusetts. After a career in science publishing in the Boston area, he began writing much more regularly: more than fifty journals and magazines have published his essays, many of which are collected in this volume, and his book *Owls Head Revisited* is out from North Country Press. Besides writing and contributing to the welfare of the Maine Turnpike, he is also president of the Board of Directors, Coastal Mountains Land Trust, in Camden, Maine.

❧

ABOUT THE ILLUSTRATOR

EMMA KROSSCHELL has been drawing and painting for most of her life. With art as a continual passion, she also has a varied background that ranges from teaching English to working in renewable energy to writing poetry. She spends much of her time outside, where her creative pursuits always find their roots. She lives in Deer Isle, Maine with her boyfriend and their dog.

CPSIA information can be obtained
at www.ICGtesting.com
Printed in the USA
LVOW03s0136110717

540912LV00004B/5/P